STRATEGIC PORTRAITS
People and Movements That
Shaped Evangelical Worship
Second Edition

STRATEGIC PORTRAITS
People and Movements That Shaped Evangelical Worship
Second Edition

Robert A. Myers

WEBBER INSTITUTE BOOKS

2019

Strategic Portraits: People and Movements that Shaped Evangelical Worship, Second Edition
ISBN-13-9781077627031
Copyright © 2019 by Robert A. Myers
WEBBER INSTITUTE BOOKS

Cover design and image by the author. Stained glass from the First Baptist Church of Galesburg, IL.

WEBBER INSTITUTE BOOKS

Webber Institute Books (WIB) serves as the publishing arm of the Robert E. Webber Institute for Worship Studies (IWS), which was founded by the late Robert E. Webber for the purpose of forming servant leaders in worship renewal with the perspective that "the way to the future necessarily runs through the past." IWS is the only school in North America dedicated solely to graduate education in biblical foundations, historical development, theological reflection, and cultural analysis of worship. Its vision emphasizes that its graduates will "participate intentionally in the story of the Triune God" in order to "bring renewal in the local and global church by shaping life and ministry according to that story." In scope it is "evangelical in nature and ecumenical in outlook, embracing and serving the whole church in its many expressions and variations." Those interested in obtaining further information concerning the Institute should consult its website at www.iws.edu.

Webber Institute Books are published in order to provide a means for disseminating to the general public varying and differing views concerning the many aspects of worship and Christian life. The ideas expressed in these published materials wholly remain the views of the authors themselves and are not necessarily those of IWS or WIB.

It is the prayerful concern of both IWS and WIB that the information contained in these works will stimulate further reflection and discussion. The results of such exchange of ideas hopefully will enhance worship renewal within the various segments of the Christian church. Moreover, in keeping with the hopes and dreams of Bob Webber, may all that is done through this publishing enterprise enable Christians to reject the narcissistic patterns prevalent in contemporary society and give the glory to God who sent Jesus, the Christ, to provide for human transformation and in concert provided humans with the divine triune presence through the Holy Spirit.

Gerald L. Borchert
Founding Editor

James Hart
President of IWS

v

List of Images

My boat at Flaming Gorge
Courtesy of Dave Myers

Charles Finney
Wikimedia Commons

Billy Sunday Preaching
Used with permission from Archives and Special Collections
Morgan Library,
Grace College and Seminary, Winona Lake, IN

Table of Contents

ENDORSEMENTS

If you've ever been to a worship service and wondered "why do we do that?" this book is for you. Myers uncovers the fascinating stories of the people and movements who have shaped the worship practices of evangelical churches in America. Even more importantly, he provides practical suggestions for worship leaders who want to build on the strengths of their evangelical worship heritage while avoiding its pitfalls. Few books combine history and practical ministry leadership advice as effectively as Myers does here.

Thomas E. Bergler, *The Juvenilization of American Christianity*
Professor of Ministry and Missions Huntington University

Bob Myers has enriched the pool of ministry resources with his thoughtful integration of select historical perspectives, theological reflection, and practical implications in light of the wider view of what God has been doing in worship since the beginning of the church. This book is insightful, engagingly written, and above all, pastoral in tone. His blend of information and reflection, rooted in decades of ministry in both the academy and the church, makes this a valuable read. I commend it to anyone serving in any type of local church ministry.

Constance M. Cherry, *The Worship Architect*
Professor of Worship and Pastoral Ministry Indiana Wesleyan University

Bob Myers walks us through the family photo album of people and movements that have shaped worship in many evangelical churches. Bob tells us how we arrived where we are so we can paint a new picture for a renewed tomorrow. Using accessible stories and engaging questions, he challenges the reader to reflect on her own perceptions and contexts. With a pastor's heart and a scholar's mind, Dr. Myers points the way to a hopeful future in congregational worship. This book is a welcome addition to anyone who wants to know the why of today's worship conversations in order to describe what a church can do in the present.

William D. Shiell
President and Professor of Pastoral Theology and Preaching
Northern Seminary

In *Strategic Portraits* Bob Myers presents a useful case that Evangelical, Free Church folks can look not only to the New Testament but also to the entire breadth of church history to find resources for renewing worship today. I applaud his boldness.

Lester Ruth
Research Professor of Christian Worship Duke Divinity School

The famous Latin phrase "Ecclesia semper reformanda est" can be translated as "The Church is always reforming." Originally attributed to St. Augustine, this phrase constitutes a call for Christians to actively participate in the ongoing renewing and reforming work of the Spirit in his Mystical Body, the Church. In the final chapter of this book Robert A. Myers wrote, "...the hope of this book is that, informed with a greater understanding of our strengths and weaknesses in corporate worship, we may begin to renew and reform our practice in order to fulfill the Kingdom mission that God has given to us in our historical moment." *Strategic Portraits* is an excellent starting point for Free Church leaders to connect with the historic church's theological and biblical development of worship. It would behoove us all to pay attention to that development as we are gathered, formed into Christlikeness, and sent on mission to love the world to the God who is perfect love.

James Hart
President, The Robert E. Webber Institute for Worship Studies

FOREWORD

It takes a gifted artistic writer to provide a genuinely perceptive and readable analysis of the streams of worship history which can both inform general Christian audiences and challenge ministers to reflect on what is being done in their churches. My former doctoral student, Robert Myers, who has since graduation been a professor, a senior pastor and a worship leader in various places, is such a person. Moreover, this book offers insightful portraits of significant contributions which varying people and movements have made to the contemporary evangelical church together with critiques and warnings concerning inappropriate and dangerous patterns in church practices. Written in flowing prose, this work of Myers will engender rethinking by those who particularly regard themselves to be within the broad spectrum of evangelicalism, but also by those from other faith communities who have influenced them and/or have been influenced by them.

This book includes many personal anecdotes that draw readers into the author's goal of shaking off the bonds of poor and ineffective worship practices and freeing Christians to consider new possibilities. Using the image of family portraits, Myers treats the complex of faith communities designated as Evangelicals and so-called "free churches" as a family and reflects on the various contributions that have impacted their church services and worship patterns.

I commend Myers for his approach because he has learned an important lesson as a Christian minister. It is that teaching theology and church practice is best presented not in formulas but in pictures. As I have indicated in my recent work on the *Portraits of Jesus for an Age of Biblical illiteracy,*[1] this use of picture-thinking or portrait-writing was the secret to communication of the divine message by Jesus and the early disciples. Jesus, God's Son, the Christ, taught in word-pictures and even behind the writings of the great Apostle Paul there usually lies picture-thinking. But the

---

[1] Gerald L. Borchert, *Portraits of Jesus for an Age of Biblical Illiteracy* (Macon, GA: Smyth & Helwys, 2016).

western church has become formula oriented and much preaching today has become point-oriented after the manner of the Greco-Roman rhetorical schools. There is, of course, an important place for logicians and as a former lawyer I am clearly aware of this reality. But I repeat, the secret of Jesus was picture-thinking. Myers has followed this pattern and the book is accordingly a fine study or text for Christian readers concerning worship.

While the author uses a rough historical outline, his interest is in issues and movements. He has provided a very helpful summary or historical review of the time between the biblical period and the Reformation, a period which many evangelicals and other Protestants are often rather unaware because they tend to jump in their thinking from the Bible to the Reformation. Then Myers' reflections into the arguments over the Table of the Lord by the Reformers should assist in providing background insights into why churches that are primarily word-oriented since the Reformation have frequently fractured. His discussion of the Pietistic Movement will also help to underscore for readers why many Evangelicals have a deep commitment to personal piety, unlike some groups who could be viewed as more "fundamentalistic"—a distinction that is frequently not recognized with respect to "Evangelicals."

But it is probable that where the book will stir periodic rereading and rethinking involves the chapters dealing with more recent movements such as the author's analyses of the legacy of Revivalism, the Jesus People Movement and the contributions of Willow Creek. These movements are well articulated by Myers since they have left an indelible mark on contemporary Evangelicalism. His summary insights and questions throughout these chapters should engender pause, observation, reconsideration and perhaps changes in current practices of churches.

The concluding chapter and the Appendices are practical in nature and reflect the experience of one who has dealt with the nature and realities of actually serving a church or faith community. Since every congregation has its own DNA, the ideas are suggestive and are not intended to be viewed as programmatic. Yet as suggestions they do not leave the reader in an ethereal no-man's land. They are intended to provide a way forward for ministers and churches that are wrestling with problematic patterns in worship practice.

Welcome, then, to reading this fine work and may God bless you in doing so.

Gerald L. Borchert
Senior Professor of New Testament,
Carson-Newman University
Emeritus Thesis Director,
The Robert E. Webber Institute for Worship Studies

PREFACE

Writing a book is a calling. At least it was for me. When I began my career as a worship pastor forty years ago, writing a book about worship was not part of my plan. Back then, I was simply devoted to my craft and passionate about the wave of change that was overtaking evangelical churches in the realm of worship. It started with those transcendent experiences in the early Jesus People Movement when we would sing Jerry Sinclair's "Alleluia." I sensed something that I had never felt before in church. God was on the move and worship was a big part of it. In the 1970's, I attended Biola College in Southern California and took a class in worship taught by Bruce Leafblad. At the time, he was the Music Minister at Lake Avenue Congregational Church in Pasadena where Ray Ortland was the Senior Minister. Something very special was happening at Lake Avenue and Leafblad brought it with him when he taught worship at Biola. He introduced me to the writings of A.W. Tozer, whose heart and pen were aflame for the glory of God. I've considered Tozer one of my spiritual "mentors" through his writings ever since then. Further, Professor Leafblad's approach to worship was traditional, incorporating the best of hymnody and liturgy and it provided the perfect counter-balance to the immersion of contemporary worship that I was experiencing with the new songs coming out of Calvary Chapel, just thirty minutes down the freeway.

The journey in my vocational calling of leading worship has been rich and varied; I weave many of my experiences into the narratives and reflections throughout *Strategic Portraits*. In 2005, I was given the unique opportunity to launch an undergraduate program in worship leadership at Huntington University in Indiana. In academia, you are encouraged to write for publication. "Publish or perish" is the mantra one hears as soon as the ink is dry on your first contract. But with all the entrepreneurial energy and imagination required in starting a new program along with learning the skills of a new career in higher education, I never seemed to have the time to begin such a project. It wasn't until I left Huntington and returned to local church ministry that I finally had time to imagine and undertake the writing of this book.

Since the beginning of my ministry, I've always been committed to worship renewal in the local church. I'm a survivor of the "worship wars." I've been targeted and wounded by both traditionalists and worship progressives. Even with the pain I experienced, I could never walk away. Worship renewal was and remains a calling for me.

I've always loved history. When students groused about taking music history at Biola, I ate it up. Graduate studies in choral music and at the Robert E. Webber Institute for Worship Studies further fed my love for history. The largest chapter in my doctoral thesis was an historical survey of devotional literature that was over seventy pages long. (IWS will no longer tolerate such an indulgence today.) I loved putting the stories together into an arch of development that informed my mind of why we do what we do today. More on that later. That's the central thesis of *Strategic Portraits*.

Along with my love for history, I've learned to enjoy writing. I don't know that I'm the best writer, but I relish the process because it clarifies my thinking. Even now, I write my sermons out in full manuscript each week because it makes me a better thinker and preacher.

So, these three things: passion for worship renewal, a love of history, and the enjoyment of writing converged to press an urgency in my spirit and mind to write this book. My earnest hope is that it will be useful as a catalyst for thoughtful discussion and action leading to worship renewal in the churches of those who read and digest what I have offered.

Each chapter includes some suggested questions at the end for reflection that would be effective in a group setting. Having taught in both undergraduate and graduate ministry settings, I believe *Strategic Portraits* would be a helpful resource as a primary or at least an auxiliary text in the classroom. Senior pastors and worship leaders would especially benefit from engaging this book together. From time to time, throughout my career as a worship pastor, I've had the opportunity to participate in local worship leader fellowships. *Strategic Portraits* would be an enjoyable and productive reading project for local or regional worship affinity groups. A few congregations are fortunate to have worship planning teams that include pastoral staff and lay leaders. Working through this book may be particularly beneficial for such a ministry team.

Every author is indebted to many people in getting his or her work published. Six years ago, when I first proposed this project, Gerald Borchert was enthusiastic about it. He wanted the manuscript ASAP and gave me a six-month deadline. Life, however, had different plans. But when I approached him five years later with a completed manuscript, he was still enthusiastic. Dr. Borchert read my manuscript, demanded that I address a critical omission that required an additional chapter, and rebuked me for dropping "the golden thread." (He was my thesis director after all; I should have known better.) If this book makes sense and holds together, it is largely due to his expert and diligent guidance. His enthusiasm for *Strategic Portraits* has been truly humbling and his generous forward for my book is a gift and affirmation for which I will always be grateful.

I would not have had the professional opportunities that have enriched my life in the last ten years if it weren't for Robert Webber, his Institute for Worship Studies, and its exceptional faculty. Webber passed away in 2007, but IWS has continued to be a source of spiritual formation and inspiration for me since I started there in 2001. When I have the opportunity to attend post-graduate seminars from time to time, it is like coming home. I'll always be very grateful to Bob and to the Institute for the deep formation that has been impressed upon me in that special place.

I'm indebted to those who have taken the time to read my manuscript and offer an endorsement of my work. All of them are recognized as exceptional scholars and leaders in their callings. I am humbled by the gift of their time and thoughtful words.

I'm a big-picture thinker. I love the forest but I often trip over trees. My good friends Pama Bennett and Mike Miller have edited my work for English grammar, style, and usage. Moreover, they graciously expressed enthusiasm for this project while correcting my innumerable grammatical indiscretions. This book would not exist without the gift of their invaluable expertise. I owe them both a debt that I cannot repay.

This book was first published in 2018 but the result was very unsatisfactory because of the many formatting errors that it contained. I'm grateful to the many people who have pointed out the problems in the first edition, especially to those who made an exhaustive list and sent it to me! I still believe that *Strategic Portraits* is an important book, so I have gone to the trouble of correcting the errors and reformatting the second edition myself.

Strategic Portraits was written over the course of six years. During that time, I changed careers as a worship pastor to become a senior pastor. We sold two homes, purchased three others, and made three job transitions within those six years. Through it all, my wife Diane has been my confidant, deepest friend, prayer and ministry partner. Life has certainly been a holy adventure together. It is to her that this book is lovingly dedicated.

Introduction
Family Pictures and Sunday Mornings

Rejoice in God's saints, today and all days;
A world without saints forgets how to praise,
Their faith in acquiring the habit of prayer,
Their depth of adoring, Lord, help us to share.
Fred Pratt Green (1903-2000)

I love family picture albums. One of my favorite activities in visiting my mom and dad after they retired was to thumb through their books of family photos. Though many of the pictures faded, I took great pleasure in rehearsing the warm memories of my childhood. As I dug a little deeper, I also found pictures of relatives I had barely known and houses where I had lived but which I could not remember. Those pictures tell a story that never loses its freshness. The story is mine. The images communicate the development of who I am – where I've lived and the people and events that have shaped my soul.

The church has a story, too. But for most modern Evangelicals, it seems that we've mislaid the photo albums. Either that, or we've never cared very much to look at them. We tend to be rootless, except for the beginning of our story which is recorded in Scripture. But to mark the end of the first century to the present, we only have a few pictures hanging on the walls – perhaps of Martin Luther, John Wesley, or D.L. Moody. On the other hand, we've got plenty of contemporary images – people with the latest fix to grow the church or gifted leaders who have built successful ministries. And the images are not just hanging on the walls or stored away in picture albums. We've made slideshows and movies out of our contemporary heroes. Just check the shelves in your local Christian bookstore and you'll find a plethora of material to help you live the Christian life.

A Crisis of Spiritual Formation

I am writing out of conviction to address the serious challenges we face as Evangelicals in American culture. I am a product of the late twentieth century, born right in the middle of the Baby Boom. As I child, I lived with the very real threat of nuclear annihilation during the sixties. "Duck and cover" was a familiar drill to me in grade school. I recall the political and social upheaval of the time. Though I was a few years too young for the draft, I felt the confusion and anger over the Vietnam War. Just as I was emerging into adulthood, I despaired at the "national malaise" of the late 1970's. I doubted that I would ever be a participant in the "American dream" – own my own home and have a family.

As I write this, the spirit of the times feels eerily like those depressing days of high inflation and unemployment in the late 70's and early 80's. The world, it seems, is on the brink of economic disaster. Our own national debt continues to explode and is more than 100% of our annual gross domestic product. The threat of terrorism seems ubiquitous and the possibility of a rogue nation acquiring nuclear weapons is a horrifying possibility. The American political system is hopelessly divided while we debate healthcare, energy, and the size of government. It is clear that we must address issues of sustainability for our planet but even that question is mired in political polarization. Capitalism is the most productive economic system the world has ever known but it has spawned crass consumerism and selfishness in all areas of our life.

The modern American evangelical church must address the challenges we face as a culture. In the past, we have maintained that for society to be changed, the sole solution is for more people to be brought to Christ. It seems that a large percentage of Americans already identify themselves as having been "brought to Christ." In Barna's *State of the Church 2016* report, 35% of

Americans claimed to be "born-again" Christians.[1] In the first three hundred years of the church, a much smaller percentage of the population claimed the name of Christ and yet they transformed the known world. But the 35% in our culture who claim to be "born-again" seem to have no noticeable distinction from the rest of the population except that they tend to be politically conservative. Marital fidelity, sexual ethics, and other markers of moral conviction seem to be indistinguishable between those who claim to be Christians and those who do not. We preach a good game, but in the end, we are no different from the rest of society. No wonder so many in our culture consider the evangelical church as irrelevant and openly express hostility towards us. We don't necessarily need more people "brought to Christ" (though I am all for evangelism); we need to be brought *into* Christ (Eph. 4:15).

How did we get to such a place of seeming impotency? As I see it, Evangelicalism and Americanism were "made for each other." Evangelicalism's emphasis on personal faith fits well with the individualism of the American spirit. I don't consider that to be an unfortunate convergence. That Evangelicalism found a ready home in the American story has been a blessing to the whole world, attested to by the missionary and ministry initiatives launched from our shores for over two hundred years. But with the convergence of individualistic values, we have been blinded to the dangers of accommodation to our culture's expectations. Evangelicals have always been a pragmatic people. We, like the Apostle Paul, would become "a servant to all, that I might more of them" (I Cor. 9:19).[2] But in our pragmatism, we have often failed to reflect and recognize how we have compromised the gospel and its mandate to make true disciples who are being formed in the image of Christ.

Evangelical Aversion to History and Tradition

---

[1] < https://www.barna.com/research/state-church-2016/> Accessed March 4, 2017.

[2] Unless otherwise noted, as Scripture quotations are from the English Standard Version (ESV).

Almost since our beginnings in the eighteenth century, Evangelicals have been dismissive of tradition. *Sola scriptura* has been our mantra. No book but the Bible. No creed but the Scriptures. Our faith is personal and spiritual, in which we rely on the Holy Spirit to guide us into all truth. We take at face value the words of the Apostle John, "...the anointing that you received from him [the Holy Spirit] abides in you, and you have no need that anyone should teach you" (I John 2:27).[3] Consequently, Evangelicals have tended to discount over two thousand years of Church tradition, maintaining that for much of that time, most of the Church was apostate.[4] There is little interest in church history for most Evangelicals. Heroes of the church are seldom mentioned in sermons or in Sunday School. My efforts to establish All Saints Day as an annual service in churches I've served have been met with suspicion and fear that it might be "too Catholic."

As participants in the American spirit and suspicious of tradition, we have also been swept up into the modern narrative of the world which was birthed in the eighteenth century. Modernism has given us the scientific revolution and all of the wonderful conveniences that we continue to enjoy. It has given us the automobile, the computer, and even taken us to the moon. But it has also elevated Reason above God and scoffs at mystery and spirituality. In its arrogance, modernism sees only today and tomorrow. History doesn't matter.

Modernism's tendency to jettison history as irrelevant has left many Evangelicals as veritable orphans, cut off from the past which has shaped us. We desperately need to find and revel in the family picture albums of church history if we are to understand ourselves fully and how to move forward in the challenging days we face. Furthermore, there is probably no enterprise of the church that more urgently needs understanding of its

---

[3] "Taking it at face value" is not always the best hermeneutic. In the passage cited, the interpreter needs to be aware of the challenge that the Apostle John was addressing – namely, know-it-all heretics who were trying to pull the church away from the true gospel (v. 26).

[4] When referring to the universal body or a specific denomination, "Church" will be capitalized. Lower case refers to a local body.

4

development than our practice of corporate worship. What we do when we regularly gather together forms us, both as individuals and as communities.

It is my conviction that the pathway of renewal in the contemporary church is first through its corporate worship. It is in corporate worship that the gospel is proclaimed and enacted. And it is the gospel that "is the power of God for salvation to everyone who believes" (Romans 1:16b). It is the gospel that has the power to change not only the church, but also the whole world. The critical question, however, is which gospel are we proclaiming and enacting in corporate worship today? That has always been the question. Whenever the whole liturgy - our songs, prayers, preaching, baptism, and Communion - have been true to the tradition handed down to us from the apostles and the written word of the Scriptures, the gospel has transformed people and society.[5] But when the church's worship practice has diluted the gospel through theological error, arrogance, exclusion, cultural accommodation, or any other distortion, it loses its transformative power. It is no longer the gospel of which the Apostle Paul was not ashamed. Cultural critic and author Nancy Pearcey explains and laments the historical process of gospel dilution that Evangelicals incurred because of our reactionary worship practices based on faulty premises:

> The troubling thing about all this is that Christianity was not shaping the culture so much as the culture was shaping Christianity. In the classic Protestant churches – Lutheran, Reformed, Anglican – corporate statements of faith such as creeds, confessions, and formal liturgies were considered necessary means of expressing communal identity and structuring communal worship. But now all theological formulations were denounced as nothing but man-made devices to keep the people "under the thumb of clerical tyrants." As liberal individualism was taking root in politics,

---

[5] An excellent source for understanding the relationship between Tradition and Scripture is *Retrieving the Tradition and Renewing Evangelicalism: A Primer for Suspicious Protestants* by D.H. Williams. (Grand Rapids, MI: William B. Eerdmans Publishing Co., 1999).

it was being uncritically applied to the churches, producing a highly individualistic and democratic ecclesiology. Modern values like autonomy and popular sovereignty became simply taken for granted in evangelical churches.[6]

Returning the church to its counter-cultural role of transformation can begin effectively through renewing its worship. But to navigate the pathway of worship renewal successfully, we must first get our bearings. An understanding of our story – the movements and events that shaped us – will enable us to locate our circumstances on the map of history.

The Focus of the Book

This book is an attempt to address the need for modern non-liturgical (Free Church[7]) worshippers to understand ourselves. I had the privilege of launching and teaching an undergraduate worship leadership program at Huntington University for five years. Part of my assignment each semester was to teach *Understanding the Christian Faith*, one of the core courses in the university's curriculum that all students were required to take. Teaching the course was one of many pleasant surprises that I had at Huntington. My favorite text was Mark Noll's *Turning Points*. While Noll only dealt with selected critical events, I found that his approach was effective in charting the flow and development of the church's history. I have adopted the same idea of selective analysis for this work, which is focused specifically on the development of Free Church worship.

---

[6] Nancy Pearcey, *Total Truth: Liberating Christianity from Its Cultural Captivity*, (Wheaton, IL: Crossway Books, 2005), 277.

[7] "Free Church" as I use the term in this work is not an institution like the association of churches known as The Evangelical Free Church, but rather churches that share common values, beginning with opposition to an established State Church and extending to opposition against any outside controlling influence on the local church. Free Churches are autonomous and as an expression of that autonomy tend to resist historic creeds or set liturgies.

There are many definitions for worship. I am defining Free Church worship as services that are characterized primarily by music and the sermon. The Lord's Table is not observed weekly. Generally, creeds are not recited, responsive readings are limited and prayers are spontaneous. Musical style is not necessarily a defining factor. Free Church worship could be either contemporary or traditional.

A book that seeks to bring understanding of a Protestant tradition will necessarily focus on Post-Reformation people and events. But before we begin our consideration of strategic portraits in the Protestant story, we will survey highlights of the first fifteen hundred years of Christian worship in Chapter One. Evangelicals have all too often ignored Early and Medieval Church history. That was certainly my experience prior to engaging in formal worship studies. Perhaps we have disregarded fifteen hundred years of our history out of arrogance or fear of being "too Catholic." In any case, we cannot consider worship developments in the Protestant Evangelical tradition without some understanding of Pre-Reformation history that has, indeed, impacted the way we worship today. Moreover, one of the significant evangelical worship renewal impulses of the twenty-first century is a reconsideration of ancient worship practices.

In Chapter Two, we will begin our consideration of formative people and events with Ulrich Zwingli's theology of the Lord's Table. His view of Communion has dominated the thought and practice of the Reformed Church and most of their non-liturgical historical heirs. In Chapter Three, I will show how Lutheran Pietist renewal efforts in the seventeenth and eighteenth centuries have impacted all Evangelicals and the way we conceptualize Christian conversion and our relationship with Christ. Perhaps the most powerful shaping movement for Free Church worship was Revivalism. In Chapter Four, I will focus on the ministry of Dwight Moody and Ira Sankey to show how they especially impacted corporate worship in the late nineteenth and early twentieth centuries. Chapter Five narrates the Praise and Worship Movement's emergence from the Jesus People Movement through my own personal perspective as a teenager and young adult living in Southern California during the 1970s. Chapter Six will address the powerful impact of the Seeker-Church Movement, using the story of Willow Creek Community Church to assess the movement's contributions and challenges to corporate worship. The final chapter summarizes the events and movements considered in the book, and offers practical components for approaching worship renewal in the local church.

One of the challenges in writing this book was to make it useful for pastors and lay persons. While I have done my homework and tried to be historically accurate in my depiction of events, I am not an historical scholar. Where appropriate, I have inserted quotes that help to illustrate my point and footnotes where necessary. But I am first and foremost a pastoral church musician. My interest is primarily in worship renewal and practice. Admittedly, I am passionate and opinionated about the topics that I am presenting. I expect that the reader may not agree with all of my conclusions and remedies. Still, if the historical backgrounds and analyses that I present provokes thoughtful reflection and action leading to worship renewal in the local church, then the objective of this project will be realized.

Throughout the book I have included personal stories from my forty years of ministry experience which relate to the issue being discussed. Each chapter will begin with a brief narrative to provide a sense that history is a living story. Principles that developed from the event or movement and impacted evangelical thought and practice in worship will be noted. I will prompt further reflection and offer ideas for contemporary renewal at the end of each chapter. Finally, I will offer suggestions for further reading on the topic.

Why Bother with History?

Why should we bother with worship history? There are at least four compelling reasons. First, just as a picture album can help us understand who we are, so worship history helps us to understand what we do and why we do it. When I taught aspiring worship leaders at Huntington, I always impressed upon them the importance of having a good reason for doing everything they plan in a worship service. I learned the same principle many years prior when I was in college. It has served me well, but it has also probably been the source of my greatest frustration. It seems that many people believe what is included in a given worship service is based on preference or ingrained practice. If that were so, we would be in a state of constant tension. Unfortunately for many, that may be the case. We all have our own preferences. We come from different traditions. How then can we plan worship services that will serve the transformational and Kingdom purposes of God? We can only fulfill that mandate by understanding what we are doing and why we do it. For many Evangelicals, it is enough to assert that we are following Scripture. But that is both naïve and arrogant. Even our approach to Scripture is shaped by the tradition in which we have been formed. We begin with Scripture so that we may order our worship practice rightly. But we need to know our unique history to understand our current circumstances. It tells us who we are.

Second, history is effective in instructing us to avoid pitfalls and inspiring us to well-doing. Throughout this work, the usefulness of worship history will be shown in this way. We are all imperfect. History has its share of rogues and heroes; we also have them today. In the pages that follow, we'll see people who, viewing things through their contemporary lens, sought to serve God and the Church well. We'll also observe how their views and actions served and, in some cases, negatively impacted how the church worshipped. Of course, the evaluations that I offer in each chapter are my own and you may not agree. But if the story and the conclusions that I draw provoke the reader to deeper reflection, this project will have served its purpose.

Third, when we view history, we can be encouraged that the church will always prevail. Christ himself promised that would always be the case (Matt. 16:18). During its first three centuries, the Church was challenged by deadly persecution and philosophies of the world like Jewish legalism and Gnosticism. Several of the New Testament epistles were written to counter the onslaughts of heretical teaching and encourage the faithful to persevere through tribulation. For example, the Arian controversy arising from within the church, which denied the full deity of Christ, threatened to tear the church apart until the

Council of Nicaea in 325 A.D. The history of the church through the Middle Ages is one of ebb and flow between decline and renewal. The Protestant Reformation of the sixteenth century coincided with a general renaissance of intellectual, social, and political life. Its effects were the most profound and lasting. But the history of Protestantism isn't perfect either. The purity and power of the gospel have been challenged by our politics, subjectivism, and sectarianism, manifested in countless battles, church splits, and heresy. The twenty-first century offers significant challenges for Evangelicals in the West. For the most part, we are declining. We are looking for spiritual traction. There is a sense of ecclesiastical vertigo. These are days that demand creativity and courage.

The Church has always been engaged in a battle for its survival and health; such challenges are not new. During the height of one those battles, Anglican pastor Samuel J. Stone penned these words:

> The Church's one foundation
> Is Jesus Christ her Lord,
> She is His new creation
> By water and the Word.
> From heaven He came and sought her
> To be His holy bride;
> With His own blood He bought her
> And for her life He died.
>
> The Church shall never perish!
> Her dear Lord to defend,
> To guide, sustain, and cherish,
> Is with her to the end:
> Though there be those who hate her,
> And false sons in her pale,
> Against both foe or traitor
> She ever shall prevail.

The church's story is one of challenge and renewal. As we face the future, we can be assured, based on Christ's promise and the testimony of history, the church will prevail.

Finally, embracing our history tells us that we are not alone. We are part of God's Grand Story of Redemption. Our Jewish forbearers in the faith understood this. Connection with the past is the reason the Hebrew Scriptures contain so many genealogies. Remembering and being dynamically connected to the Story is the rationale and mandate for observing all the Jewish feasts. The New Testament Church and the early Church Fathers understood their connection to the past as well. It is the reason New Testament writers quote the Old Testament so much. The Church Fathers always appealed to the Hebrew Scriptures and the apostolic tradition (II Thess. 2:15). The Protestant Reformers, in their efforts to renew the church, appealed not only to Scripture but also to the history and tradition passed down by the Church Fathers.[8] Knowing and embracing our historical story is the prescription for the modern malaise of arrogance that jettisons tradition and lusts after novelty. Our history connects us with the likes of Luther, Zwingli, Wesley, Jonathan Edwards, D.L. Moody, and countless others who "served God in their generation." We are part of a much larger story – a family that spans the globe and for all time. History connects us not only to our past, but also to our future and compels us to consider what our legacy will be for generations of worshippers.

It's time to break out the family picture albums.

Questions for Reflection:

1. How has your family history formed you?

2. Is the American evangelical church in crisis? In what ways? How can a renewal of corporate worship address our challenges?

3. How much history of your own church tradition do you know?

---

[8] Williams, 180-194.

4. Have you ever heard a sermon or had a Sunday School class that explored church history? Why do you suppose that might be the case?

5. Do you feel connected to believers from an earlier era? Why or why not?

For Further Reading:

Noll, Mark A., *Turning Points: Decisive Moments in the History of Christianity, 32nd Edition,* (Grand Rapids, MI: Baker Academic, 2012).

Phillips, Timothy R. and Okholm, Dennis L., *A Family of Faith: An Introduction to Evangelical Christianity,* (Grand Rapids, MI: Baker Academic, 2001).

Tanner, Kenneth and Hall, Christopher A., eds., *Ancient and Postmodern Christianity: Paleo-Orthodoxy in the 21st Century, Essays in Honor of Thomas C. Oden,* (Downers Grove, IL: Intervarsity Press, 2002).

Webber, Robert E., *Ancient-Future Worship: Proclaiming and Enacting God's Narrative,* (Grand Rapids, MI: Baker Books, 2008).

Williams, D.H., *Retrieving the Tradition and Renewing Evangelicalism: A Primer for Suspicious Protestants,* (Grand Rapids, MI: William B. Eerdmans Publishing Co., 1999).

Willimon, William H., *Word, Water, Wine and Bread: How Worship Has Changed Over the Years,* (Valley Forge, PA: Judson Press, 1980).

Historical Ballast

Faith of our fathers,
Holy faith!
We will be true
To thee till death!
Frederick W. Faber, 1849

I was born into a nautical family. One doesn't have to turn too many pages in the Myers family picture album before boats begin to appear. My paternal grandfather was a ship's carpenter like his father. By the time he was eighteen, he had built his own sloop and sailed it solo around Long Island, New York. He spent most of his career in a private yard, building and repairing wooden boats in Bayport, NY. My father, on the other hand, loved airplanes and became an aeronautical electrician. But the boat-building bug bit him, too. There was a time when our family had nine boats in our garage or yard that he had built. One of my two brothers is a wooden-boat builder *par excellence,* now retired from teaching so that he can devote more time to his craft.

I didn't catch the apple when it fell from the tree. My best efforts are in miniature: wooden models or ships-in-bottles. Still, I love boats and sailing. Several years ago, my boat-building brother convinced me to buy a fifteen-foot rowing dory from him. (Dories are typically "double-ended" boats with flat bottoms and flared sides.) It was a beautiful and stoutly-built vessel. After I had owned it for a while, I decided that I wanted to add a sailing rig. I purchased an antique book on how to make sails and I proceeded to make my set from sturdy canvas. It was a great project. I followed the old craft of sail-making, including broad-seaming and hand-stitched roping to produce a set of sails that impressed even my brother. I made the spars and installed the mast footing on the boat.

I well remember her maiden voyage. It was a rather blustery midwestern day; the wind was probably sustaining around 15 MPH. I loaded up the boat and took her to Brown's Lake near Sioux City, Iowa. I put up the rigging and admired my handiwork and the beauty of her lines. I felt like a real Myers. When I pushed off from the dock, it was rather slow going for a few minutes because the wind was light close to shore. But when I got out to the middle of the lake, she nearly capsized! I had to let go of all the controlling ropes to depower the sail, watching it flap violently in the wind. It was a great day for sailing but my boat couldn't handle it! Humiliated and greatly disappointed, I pulled the mast and sails down, got out my oars, and rowed back to the dock.

My boat at Flaming Gorge, Wyoming

I called my brother to ask for advice and he took me to task for making a solid-core mast and using too heavy sailcloth. He was still the top-dog in our boat-building clan. I called my dad and he said I needed to put some ballast in the bottom of the boat. Looking back, I realized that any good sailor would know that. The following week, I took the two 70-pound sandbags that I used for traction in my truck and put them in the bottom of the dory. She sailed beautifully. In fact, the last time I sailed the boat, she performed wonderfully with my brother serving as crew and "ballast."

14

Like my boat on that windy day at Brown's Lake, Evangelicals often try to navigate their way without the benefit of historical ballast. We scan the wind and the waves of our cultural context and then rig our ecclesiastical ship with theology, methodology, and practical programs that look really nice at first glance. But when we fail to consider the weight of our long history and tradition, we run the risk of being overwhelmed and overturned when we launch out to engage the world. We need the ballast of historical perspective.

For most of my life, I understood the history of the Church through a narrative that seemed to project the following:

1. The New Testament Church got it all right.
2. The Church stayed fairly pure through its first three centuries, as evidenced by its perseverance under persecution, but quickly apostasized after the faith became the official religion of the Roman Empire.
3. Nothing positive happened in the Church from the fourth century until the Reformation in the early sixteenth century.
4. The Church returned to its early roots and purity after the Reformation.

Of course, the NT Church did not always "get it right." Correction was a subject in many of the epistles. The seven churches of Revelation did not survive. And the years between the Council of Nicaea (325 A.D) and the Reformation (1517 A.D.) brought many positive developments that affect us even today. Certainly, not all Protestants or even those from my Baptist tradition would hold such a narrow view as I was taught. But I'm sure that the perspective I held is rather pervasive throughout Free Churches.

When we omit twelve hundred years of church history from the Ante-Nicene Church (pre-325 A.D.) to the Protestant Reformation, we are discarding important understanding of people and events that brought us to our current state. There are lessons to be learned, warnings to be taken, and inspiration to be had in the happenings that occurred in the Church during that long period. It is true that modern Evangelicalism is a Protestant tradition. Post-Reformation history, therefore, will be the focus of this book. But in the following pages, I will highlight some of the people and movements that shaped our understanding and practice of worship leading up to the Reformation and lasting until today.

The Ante-Nicene Worship (Pentecost – 325 A.D.)

Worship in the New Testament Church
The New Testament does not give us specific prescriptions as to how we are to order Christian corporate worship. The most direct instructions given regarding public worship are found in I Corinthians where the Apostle Paul takes the church to task for abuses at the Lord's Table and for their disorderly use of spiritual gifts. But there are no complete orders of worship to be found in the Gospels, Acts of the Apostles, or the Epistles. Instead, we have a few "snapshots" of corporate worship through descriptions and instructions regarding specific elements in their gatherings.

The first description of Christian worship in Acts 2:42 is perhaps the most well-known and referenced verse regarding the nature of the corporate Church. Luke records that the newly-formed Church "devoted themselves to the apostles' teaching and the fellowship, to the breaking of bread and the prayers" (ESV). Later, as the Church would develop and "the apostles' teaching" would be distributed in the written form of the four Gospels and the NT Epistles, gathered churches would hear the teaching through public readings. Throughout Luke's narrative in Acts, we observe that the Church shared life together through fellowship, including material resources and support for those in need. We understand from Paul's corrective to the Church in I Corinthians 11 that believers typically observed the Lord's Table within the larger context of a shared meal together. The New Testament does not seem to indicate whether prayer or "prayers" were a singular event within corporate worship like the reading of Scriptures, preaching, teaching (I Tim. 4:1), or the Lord's Table. Prayer is saturated throughout each of the books of the New

Testament. It is possible that there was a focused "prayer event" (like our "pastoral prayer") in the worship gatherings of the first century. But it is also likely that prayer was integrated throughout the full worship service.

The New Testament Church began as a Jewish sect in Jerusalem. Their conception of a religious gathering would have emerged from their experience in the synagogue. Reading from the Scriptures, followed by exhortation and teaching, naturally became a central event for the fledgling Church. But in contrast to the Jewish synagogue, the Christians added the element of a meal – most importantly, a meal of remembrance, the Lord's Table.

> *They devoted themselves to the apostle's teaching and the fellowship, to the breaking of bread and the prayers.* **(Acts 2:42)**

The primary pattern of corporate worship that emerged in the first century consisted of word and table with prayers and (likely) singing integrated throughout. Singing in worship with "psalms and hymns and spiritual songs" is mentioned twice in Paul's epistles (Eph. 5:19 and Col. 3:16). Outside of corporate worship, Luke records that Paul and Silas sang in the Philippian jail (Luke 16:25). Paul references singing in I Cor. 14:15 and it is also mentioned in James 5:13. The worship narrative in Revelation 4 and 5 is saturated with song. Even though there is little mention of singing in worship instructions or descriptions in the New Testament, it is reasonable to assume that song, along with prayer, was characteristic of New Testament corporate worship.

Early Church Descriptions

In the second and third centuries following the establishment of the Church, little appears to have changed in the essential structure of word and table interspersed with prayers and song. Most of the primitive churches met in homes and often faced the challenge of persecution. They had little opportunity or resources to elaborate their corporate worship experience, not that any elaboration or development was necessary. The first three centuries of the Church witnessed explosive growth across the Roman Empire.

The few sources that we have from the Ante-Nicene Period reaffirm the notion that Christian corporate worship remained rather simple, anchored in the two primary events of word and table. The *Didache*[1], which dates around the turn of the first century, offers descriptions and instructions regarding the Christian Faith, principles of church life, and corporate worship. Notably, it references teaching, praying the Lord's Prayer, and prayers for Communion. Justin Martyr's *Apology*, dating from about 150, offers this description of typical Christian worship at the time:

> The day that is commonly called Sunday all those [believers] who live in the cities or fields gather, and in their meetings as much as time allows is read from the *memoirs of the apostles* or from the writings of the prophets. Then, once the reader is through, the one presiding offers a verbal exhortation, urging us to follow these beautiful examples. Immediately after this, we all stand as one and raise our prayers, after which – as I have already said – bread, wine, and water are offered, and the president, as he is able, also sends to God his prayers and thanksgiving, and all the people respond, "Amen." Now follows the distribution and partaking of the nourishment that has been consecrated by thanksgiving, and they are sent by means of the deacons to those who are not present. Those who can stand and will, freely give what seems best to them, and the offering is given to the president. With this he helps orphans and widows, those who are in need…We hold this general gathering on Sunday, because it is the

---

[1] The *Didache (The Teaching of the Twelve)* is considered to be the earliest extra-biblical description of Christian worship. Scholarly consensus dates it around 100 A.D. Several of the Church Fathers reference it in their writings. An excellent source for translations and more information can be found at http://www.earlychristianwritings.com/didache.html. Accessed July 11, 2017.

first day, in which God, transforming darkness and matter, created the world, and also the day in which Jesus Christ, our Savior, rose from the dead.[2]

The essential elements of word and table are clearly seen along with significant prayer throughout. While song is not mentioned, its absence need not necessarily be assumed through the omission in Justin's description. It is possible, however, that the practice of singing may have been diminished out of necessity in some settings because of persecution or other challenges. The mention of a weekly offering for the poor in corporate worship is also important to note.

The occurrence of word and table with prayer is found throughout all descriptions of Christian worship during this period. There were, however, some slight differences in liturgies from region to region regarding prayers and other matters. There was no single set liturgy for all the churches. Rather, certain stylistic differences arising from cultural paradigms can be found, for example, between a Syrian and a Roman liturgy.[3] While the two-fold structure of worship (word and table) was universally the same, churches utilized styles that resonated with their cultural context.

Other liturgical documents from the period reinforce the preeminence of word and table in Christian corporate worship. Of special note is *The Apostolic Tradition of Hippolytus* (c. 230) that contains a beautiful narrative Eucharistic prayer. Given that individuals did not possess personal copies of the Gospels and that many in the congregation might be illiterate, long prayers which rehearsed the fullness of Christ's mission, death, resurrection, and ascension were very effective in the spiritual formation of the Church. Hippolytus' ancient prayer creates the

---

[2] http://www.earlychristianwritings.com/text/justinmartyr-firstapology.html. CHAPTER LXVII – Weekly worship of the Christians. Accessed August 11, 2017.

[3] Lloyd G. Patterson, "The Worship of the Early Church" in Robert E. Webber, ed., *The Complete Library of Christian Worship, Vol. II: Twenty Centuries of Christian Worship* (Peabody, MA: Hendrickson Publishers, Inc., 1994) 34-35.

basis of Eucharistic prayers in Catholic, Anglican, and Lutheran liturgies today:

> The Lord be with you.
> *And all reply:*
> And with your spirit.
> *The bishop says:*
> Lift up your hearts.
> *The people respond:*
> We have them with the Lord.
> *The bishop says:*
> Let us give thanks to the Lord.
> *The people respond:*
> It is proper and just.

The bishop then continues:

We give thanks to you God, through your beloved son Jesus Christ, whom you sent to us in former times as Savior, Redeemer, and Messenger of your Will, who is your inseparable Word, through whom you made all, and in whom you were well-pleased, whom you sent from heaven into the womb of a virgin, who, being conceived within her, was made flesh, and appeared as your Son, born of the Holy Spirit and the virgin.

It is he who, fulfilling your will and acquiring for you a holy people, extended his hands in suffering, in order to liberate from sufferings those who believe in you.

Who, when he was delivered to voluntary suffering, in order to dissolve death, and break the chains of the devil, and tread down hell, and bring the just to the light, and set the limit, and manifest the resurrection,

Taking the bread, and giving thanks to you, said,
"Take, eat, for this is my body which is broken for you."
Likewise the chalice, saying,
This is my blood which is shed for you.
Whenever you do this, do this (in) memory of me.

Therefore, remembering his death and resurrection, we offer to you the bread and the chalice, giving thanks to you, who has made us worthy to stand before you and to serve as your priests. And we pray that you would send your Holy Spirit to the oblation of your Holy Church.

In their gathering together, give to all those who partake of your holy mysteries the fullness of the Holy Spirit, toward the strengthening of the faith in truth, that we may praise you and glorify you, through your Son Jesus Christ, through whom to you be glory and honor, Father and Son, with the Holy Spirit, in your Holy Church, now and throughout the ages of the ages. *Amen.*

The Importance of Creedal Statements.
It is clear through virtually every New Testament epistle that keeping the understanding and practice of the Church aligned with apostolic teaching was a constant challenge. At first, the faith was passed on primarily through oral tradition. Later, of course, the four Gospels were written along with the epistles to support and correct the churches. To meet the challenge of guarding and passing on orthodoxy, the Church developed short statements that summarized essential truths of the faith. The New Testament provides some evidence that the fledgling Church used these creedal statements to combat heresy. The earliest creedal statement, "Jesus is the Christ," would have resonated with the first Jewish converts. The emphasis on Jesus as the Jewish Messiah is evident in the first sermons in the Book of Acts. As the gospel spread to the Gentiles, the emphasis was more on affirming that "Jesus Christ is Lord." Of course, such a claim was counter-cultural, perhaps even seditious, in the Roman Empire which asserted that Caesar was Lord. These short statements concerning the nature and mission of Jesus Christ are found throughout Acts, the epistles, and Revelation. It is fair to assume that these words were on the lips of Christians both within and outside of their corporate worship gatherings.

The New Testament epistles also give evidence of more fully developed creedal statements. Clearly, I Timothy 3:16 is a case in point:

> Great indeed, we confess, is the mystery of godliness:
> He was manifested in the flesh,
> vindicated by the Spirit,
> seen by angels,
> proclaimed among the nations,
> believed on in the world,
> taken up in glory.

Paul's resurrection narrative at the beginning of I Corinthians 15 is also a statement that likely could have been easily memorized and recited together:

> For I delivered to you as of first importance what I also received: that Christ died for our sins in accordance with the Scriptures, that he was buried, that he was raised on the third day in accordance with the Scriptures, and that he appeared to Cephas, then to the twelve. Then he appeared to more than five hundred brothers at one time, most of whom are still alive, though some have fallen asleep. Then he appeared to James, then to all the apostles (v. 3-7).

The reference to the Aramaic name, "Cephas," rather than "Peter," suggests that the statement may have even pre-dated Paul's missionary journeys.[4] In addition to these clear creedal statements in the New Testament, there are other passages that seem to be more hymn-like, yet carry the same essential doctrinal themes. The *kenosis* passage in Philippians 2:6-11 and the Christological poem in Colossians 1:15-20 are often cited by scholars as examples.

Beyond the New Testament, creedal statements were especially important in baptismal liturgies. Indeed, creedal formulas likely

---

[4] Ralph P. Martin, *Worship in the Early Church*, (Grand Rapids: William B. Eerdmans Publishing Company, 1974, reprint, 2001) 58-59.

served as a "curriculum" for pre-baptismal instruction (catechism). Justin Martyr, Irenaeus (c. 130-200 A.D.), and Hippolytus described baptismal confessions in their writings. The confession that Hippolytus cites finds a clear echo in the early *Roman Creed* (340) which eventually evolved into the *Apostle's Creed* which is still in wide use today.

Church historian Mark Noll maintains that it was these ancient creedal statements, along with the formation of the New Testament Canon and the hierarchy of Church bishops, that held the early Church true to its mission and orthodox teaching.[5] The ancients knew what many modern Evangelicals might well want to reconsider in corporate worship: *regular repetition forms the mind and spirit.*

The ancients knew what many Evangelicals might well want to reconsider in corporate worship

Post-Nicene Worship (325-600 A.D.)

Major changes in the relationship between the Church and the Roman Empire occurred early in the fourth century. Constantine, who had just defeated his brutal rival, Maxentius, at the Battle of Milvian Bridge near Rome in October, 312 A.D., met with Licinius, his rival from the eastern region of the Empire. Constantine was already predisposed to offer favor to the Church as he had observed its expansion throughout the Empire, its good effect on general society, and the decline of Greco-Roman paganism. According to legend, his positive predisposition towards the faith was strengthened by the appearance of a Christian symbol prior to his battle with Maxentius, with the admonition, *"Hoc vince!"* ("By this conquer!") From his meeting with Licinius, an act of toleration for all religions was agreed upon and issued as the so-called "Edict of Milan" in January, 313. For

---

[5] Mark A. Noll, *Turning Points: Decisive Moments in the History of Christianity*, (Grand Rapids: Baker Academic, 2012, Third Edition) 25-36.

Constantine, it was pure political pragmatism. Christianity was gaining influence over paganism throughout the Empire. He saw the "handwriting on the wall."

By 324, Constantine had conquered Licinius and become the unquestioned ruler of the Empire. Alarmed by the deep division of the Church over the question of Christ's divinity and the controversy's direct threat to imperial peace, the Emperor ordered 230 bishops to gather at Nicaea and come to theological agreement. The Council of Nicaea would affirm in 325. that Christ was indeed divine and establish the doctrine of the Trinity. Aside from the important theological boundaries that were set at the Council, the fact that a secular ruler exercised authority over Church leadership set both Church and State on a mutual course that would impact both, for better and for worse, for the next millennia.

While Christianity did not become the official religion of the empire until the reign of Theodosius in 380, the effects on corporate worship through the alignment of the Church with the State after the Council of Nicaea were radical and immediate. Prior to the fourth century, most churches met in simple homes. Very few owned property. From its necessary secrecy, the faith had spread mostly through the lower classes of society rather than the highly visible privileged classes. When Christianity gained sanction from the Empire, it came out of the shadows and transformed its worship practice to meet the cultural tastes and preferences of the powerful:

> Now it came forth from its secrecy in private houses, deserts, and catacombs, to the light of day, and must adapt itself to the higher classes and the great mass of the people, who had been bred in the traditions of heathenism. The development of the hierarchy and the enrichment of public worship go hand in hand. A republican and democratic constitution demands simple manners and customs;

aristocracy and monarchy surround themselves with a formal etiquette and brilliant court-life.[6]

From the middle of the fourth century, the Church's services would become adorned by increasingly lavish houses of worship, clergy vestments and privilege, and an expanded worship order. The simple worship of the primitive Church based on word and table evolved into a four-fold structure of gathering, word, table, and sending, joined together with more elaborate prayer and song.

As the Church experienced more freedom through toleration and establishment, open celebrations of Christian feast days became more prominent. From as early as the second century, Christians had observed Easter through the baptism of new converts and first Communion. Late in the fourth century, observance expanded to a celebration of Holy Week, beginning on Palm Sunday. A remarkable pilgrimage journal by a young woman named Egeria describes elaborate celebrations throughout the week in Jerusalem around 384. The Church celebrated its birthday and baptized those converts who hadn't been ready for Easter on Pentecost Sunday, just fifty days after Holy Week. The feasts of Epiphany and, later, Christmas also emerged about the same time. By the end of the fourth century, the primary feasts of the Church year were well-established. The institution of Lent and Advent as forty-day seasons of preparation for all Christians soon followed.

Evangelicals have tended to look with disdain upon the developments that happened in the Church during and after the fourth century. We've had good reason. The establishment of Christianity as the State religion led to widespread nominalism - Christian in name only, without true heart religion. The alliance of Church and State brought the temptations of power to Church leaders, often with devastating spiritual results. The celebration of Christian feast days sometimes led to pagan debauchery, which several of the Church Fathers denounced.[7] The deep symbolism

---

[6] Philip Schaff, *History of the Christian Church, Vol. 3: Nicene and Post-Nicene Christianity, A.D. 311-590* (Peabody, MA: Hendrickson Publishers Marketing, LLC, reprint of the Fifth Edition, 1889) 375.

[7] Schaff, 392.

intended for the worship adornments that were added in the fourth century was sometimes lost in imperial pomp and splendor.

The tendency of Evangelicals to criticize the post-Nicene Church, however, has also obscured the good things that developed during this period. Observance of the Church Year is helpful in forming the Christian story in the minds and hearts of people. For Evangelicals, a full grasp and observance of the Church Year would help us understand that God has brought us into *his* Story rather than our primary focus on God being invited into *ours*.[8] In addition, recovery of the deep meanings of the developed liturgy and symbols of the period would enrich evangelical worship understanding and spiritual formation. Indeed, many Evangelicals today are rediscovering the richness of liturgy through the ancient evangelical stream of worship renewal.[9]

> **The tendency of Evangelicals to criticize the post-Nicene Church…has also obscured the good things that developed during this period.**

As early as the third century, there were men and women who separated themselves from society in order to devote themselves to a deeper spiritual life. As the Church developed beyond the fourth century, the separatist impulse became stronger in reaction to growing nominalism and other factors. Some lived solitary lives while others gathered in communities. Some engaged in radical asceticism, depriving and punishing their bodies to gain spiritual advancement. Benedict (c. 480-c. 550 A.D.) stands as a giant in the monastic movement. Around 529, he founded a community of monks south of Rome at Monte Cassino that remains to this

---

[8] The popular worship song, *Lord, I Lift Your Name on High*, illustrates this point perfectly: "Lord, I lift your name on high. Lord, I love to sing your praises. *I'm so glad you're in my life…*" (emphasis mine). By Rick Founds, © 1989 Universal Music – Brentwood Benson Publishing.

[9] See Appendix B: *The Call to An Ancient Evangelical Futur*

day. It was at this monastery that Benedict founded the order that bears his name and wrote his *Rule* that regulated the rhythm and life of his monks and nuns. *Benedict's Rule* became a standard which other monastic orders would copy in founding their communities. *The Rule* established a rhythm of prayer, work, and study for the spiritual community. Typically, regular prayer meetings, called the "hours" or "offices," were held throughout the day and evening. Modern author, Phyllis Tickle, effectively culled together material from monastic offices into a devotional manual called *The Divine Hours* for morning, noon, and evening prayer.[10] *The Divine Hours* would be a good introduction for Evangelicals who might wish to explore liturgical prayer in a personal or small group setting.

Mark Noll identifies the monastic movement as an essential force in saving Western Civilization and the Church throughout the Middle Ages.[11] He makes a compelling case. It was the monasteries that copied and preserved not only the Scriptures, but the great literary works of antiquity. Monks and nuns developed agricultural methods and established hospitals. They were also the creative and preservative force behind much of the music and arts throughout the long Dark and Middle Ages. When spirituality waned, it was the monasteries that raised up men and women to call the Church back to faithfulness.

Pope Gregory the Great and the Institutionalization of Church Music
Pope Gregory the Great (c. 540-604 A.D.) was a Benedictine monk and a giant among leaders of the Church. He was a man of spiritual integrity, supremely gifted as a leader, and remarkably humble. His accomplishments in serving the people and the Church were many, but he is probably best known for his establishment of the church music which bears his name: Gregorian Chant. He wrote a collection of poetry and songs for liturgical use and established a school for singers which became a model for other monastic orders and churches.

---

[10] Published in 2000, *The Divine Hours* is a three-volume set: Autumn/Winter, Springtime, and Summer. The offices integrate liturgical prayers and Scripture readings into a short devotional.
[11] Noll, 77-97.

During Gregory's time and for the next nearly five hundred years, Gregorian Chant, or plainchant, was an oral tradition. It should not be assumed that plainchant was sung only by trained monastic singers. It is likely that choirs were used to lead liturgical singing for the congregation. But with the development of musical notation and polyphony (multiple parts at the same time) in the eleventh century, presentational church music without the participation of the congregation began to emerge. Interestingly, Gregory's plainchant would be the primary melodic material that composers would employ for early liturgical choral works. By the twelfth and thirteenth centuries, composers were writing complex music for the liturgy that could only be performed by trained singers. The development of choirs for presentation, however, did not entirely exclude congregational singing. Simple chants and hymns were still sung by the congregation, assisted by the choir.

The development of polyphonic church music had both positive and negative effects. The negative was that choral music became increasingly complex, obscuring the simple meaning of the text. Periodically, Church hierarchy would admonish composers to simplify their works. The richness of the performance literature could also develop an ethos in the congregation of passive observance rather than active participation. This is a danger and challenge, of course, that modern Evangelicals know well, which will be addressed in Chapter Five. It is also true, however, that Western Culture owes a great debt to the Church for the development of music from the late Middle Ages through the Baroque period. For over five hundred years, the best and most sophisticated music in Europe was being written for the Church. Most of the great choral treasures of the Renaissance through the Baroque Period were written for the glory of God and for use in the Church. All choral composers and musicians, in a sense, are indebted to Pope Gregory the Great.

Medieval Worship (600-1500 A.D.)

Bernard of Clairvaux and the Mystic Tradition

Since the beginning of the monastic movement, mystic contemplation of the believer's union with God has been an essential theme in Christian tradition. The early Church Father, Origen (c. 185-254 A.D.), was arguably the most important mystic theologian until the eleventh century. His allegorical approach to the Song of Solomon has been influential through nearly eighteen hundred years. Augustine (354-430) and Dionysius the Areopagite (c. 475-525) followed Origen and developed his theology of spiritual *eros* even more.[12] It was Bernard of Clairvaux (1090-1153), however, who was the most-read mystical theologian through his multi-volume sermons and commentary on the first two chapters of the Song.

Bernard's legacy was far-reaching. Luther regarded him as the most pious and preferred of all the monks.[13] Calvin quoted Bernard's *Sermons on the Canticles* extensively in his *Institutes*.[14] Several hymns have been attributed to him, two of which are included in many hymnals today. "O Sacred Head Now Wounded," also known as "The Passion Chorale," is well-known by Evangelicals who have basic hymn literacy. "Jesus, the Very Thought of Thee" is perhaps less known, but is one of remarkable beauty:

> Jesus, the very thought of thee with sweetness fills the breast;
> but sweeter far thy face to see, and in thy presence rest.
> O hope of every contrite heart, O joy of all the meek,
> to those who fall, how kind thou art! How good to those who seek!

---

[12] No doubt following the allegorical interpretation of the Song of Solomon from Origen, Dionysius used the specific term, *eros,* for yearning for God.

[13] John Michael Talbot, *The Way of the Mystics: Ancient Wisdom for Experiencing God Today,* (San Francisco: Jossey-Bass, 2005) 33.

[14] Dennis E. Tamburello, *Bernard of Clairvaux,* (New York: The Crossroad Publishing Company, 2000) 95-101.

But what to those who find? Ah, this no tongue nor pen can show;
the love of Jesus, what it is, none but his loved ones know.

Jesus, our only joy be thou, as thou our prize wilt be;
Jesus, be thou our glory now, and through eternity.

A long train of mystics followed Bernard: Hildegarde of Bingen (1098-1179), St. Francis of Assisi (1182-1226), St. Bonaventura (1221-1274), St. Thomas Aquinas (1226-1274), Meister Eckhart (1260-1327), Richard Rolle (c. 1300-1349), and Julian of Norwich (1343-1413). The passionate devotion of the mystics influenced many of the reformers. The Pietists of the seventeenth and eighteen centuries, the topic of Chapter Three of this book, were especially impacted by the mystical devotion of these Medieval saints.

The Fourth Lateran Council
On Christmas Day, 800 A.D., Pope Leo III crowned the Frankish Ruler, Charlemagne, as "the great and peace-giving emperor of the Romans."[15] Charlemagne's coronation was symbolic of the growing interdependence between Church and State since Constantine. Christendom was fully affirmed on that day. For the next seven hundred years, every person under the rule of the Holy Roman Emperor was both citizen and Christian. Baptism was not only an act of initiation into the family of faith, but also a civic matter as well. Both the Church and State ruled as one over their subjects.

---

[15] Noll, 101.

The height of the Church's power was expressed when Pope Innocent III called the Fourth Lateran Council together in November, 1215. At the Council, which included over 1200 clergy and various heads of State, important rulings concerning the inquisition of heretics and the call for another Crusade were issued. Most importantly for corporate worship, however, the doctrine of transubstantiation was established. The Catholic Church had long believed in Christ's *real presence* at the Table. But the Fourth Lateran Council determined the mechanism - the words of institution (*"Hoc est corpus meum:* this is my body*"*) - that would change the substance from bread and wine into Christ's body and blood. Furthermore, the Council affirmed there was no possibility of salvation without this "formula" being said by the priest and the transformed elements being received by the worshipper.

...the lingering effect of the Council's dogma of transubstantiation was to cultivate fear of desecration of the elements in the minds of worshippers.

The issues regarding Christ's presence at the Table will be discussed in the next chapter. But the lingering effect of the Council's dogma of transubstantiation was to cultivate fear of desecration of the elements in the minds of worshippers. Consequently, many rarely received Communion except once a year, as required by the Church. Furthermore, the Eucharist increasingly became a "show" that the priest performed, reinforcing the Old Testament concept of the Lord's Table being a fresh sacrifice each time it was observed.

Pre-Reformation Rumblings
Nothing in human history happens in a vacuum except, of course, natural disasters. The factors leading up to and into the Reformation were many and varied. With the Renaissance (fourteenth to sixteenth century) came the rise of humanism and yearning for economic and political freedom. The heavy hand of

the Church and State alliance had worn thin in many emerging nation-states. The rise of the Islamic Ottoman Empire requiring military response in the East kept the Holy Roman Emperor distracted from giving his full attention to dissidents. The burden of the guilt-inducing theology of the Church and its scandalous selling of indulgences would fester into a boil that was eventually lanced by a feisty Wittenberg monk in 1517. Additionally, the timely invention of Gutenberg's printing press in 1440 ensured that ideas counter to the Church and State could be distributed to a restless populace.

Before the Reformation was launched by Luther, two courageous churchmen broke up the hard political and theological ground to plant the seeds of radical change. John Wycliffe (1330-1384) has been called the "Morningstar of the Reformation" because he was the first to challenge the power of the Church and Pope effectively. He was an English scholar and clergyman who would often side with national interests against the Church's official policies. He denied the infallibility of the Pope, resisted the Church's call for another holy war, challenged the offering of indulgences, and had no use for the confessional. He believed that laypeople should have access to the Scriptures in their native tongue and set about translating the Bible from Latin into English. Furthermore, in what seems obvious to Evangelicals today but was radical for his time, he insisted that the Scriptures were more authoritative than the Church. In the arena of corporate worship, he challenged the doctrine of transubstantiation.

His views were intolerable for the Church's leaders. He was branded a heretic and they set out to silence him. Wycliffe was willing to die for his beliefs but was not destined to become a martyr. Never a man of vibrant health, he experienced a paralyzing stroke in 1382. If he had the strength, he would have willingly defended himself before the Pope. Instead, he suffered another episode and died two years later. Wycliffe was very influential and inspired a great deal of hatred from his ecclesiastical opponents. In an effort to expunge his legacy, they banned his books, dug up his remains from the Church cemetery, burned them, and scattered them to the wind.

Wycliffe's influence, however, did not diminish and was not limited to England. His writings and teachings became known on the European continent where John Huss (1369-1415) adopted and spread them in Bohemia. Huss' profile as a scholar and churchman was like Wycliffe's. Like his English forerunner, he opposed the infallibility of the Pope, held to the authority of Scripture over Church decree, and questioned the doctrine of transubstantiation. Huss, however, met a different end than Wycliffe. He

Through [Huss']
death, the roots of the
Reformation began to
run deep into the rich
soil of the European
Renaissance.

was promised safe passage to the Council of Constance (1414-1415) where he hoped to present a fair defense of his views. That opportunity was never given to him. Instead, he was imprisoned under deplorable conditions for seven months, publicly humiliated, condemned, and burned at the stake on July 6, 1415. Huss's martyrdom watered the seeds of dramatic change that Wycliffe had planted forty years earlier. Through his death, the roots of the Reformation began to run deep into the rich soil of the European Renaissance until new life burst forth for the Church in little more than a hundred years.

A Divided Church:
Worship in the Four Streams of the Reformation

All Protestant reformers agreed upon several matters regarding corporate worship. They believed that the Catholic Mass had become distorted as an act of ritual sacrifice rather than of remembrance and thanksgiving. It was deemed a legalistic way of securing one's salvation without necessary faith. Though their views on the *real presence* of Christ during Communion differed, they all rejected the "mechanics" of transubstantiation. The reformers also sought to restore the preached Word to a place of prominence within corporate worship. Finally, they all believed that worship should be accessible to the people with Scripture reading, song,[16] and preaching presented in the people's language.

The fundamental difference between the four streams of the Reformation was over continuity with their Roman Catholic heritage. Martin Luther did not wish to start a new Church. He wanted to reform it. But the Catholic Church would not adopt his reforms, while the political rulers of the German States embraced them. The Lutherans, then, retained much of the liturgy of the Catholic Mass. The most significant differences were Luther's concept of *real presence* at the Eucharist, preaching and Scripture in the German tongue, and a strong heritage of vernacular song that remains to this day.

The Church of England, or the Anglican Church, was established through the English Act of Supremacy in 1534 A.D. when King Henry VIII, with the support of his Archbishop, Thomas Cranmer, and Parliament declared independence from Rome. Like the Lutherans, the Anglicans retained much of the liturgy of the Mass in their own language. Thomas Cranmer's *Book of Common Prayer,* for corporate and private worship as well as special services is a remarkable treasure in its beauty of expression and saturation of Scripture. The Anglican view of *real presence* is not clearly defined, though it is affirmed, and the "mechanical" methodology of transubstantiation is rejected. Anglicans have historically adopted an irenic posture of toleration, so within the stream there are those congregations that observe the liturgy formally (with clerical vestments, for example) and those who reject high ceremony.

It is ironic that the Reformed and Anabaptist streams shared much in common in their corporate worship values. The early Anabaptists were persecuted harshly by their Reformed counterparts, particularly because of their practice of believer's

---

[16] Zwingli was a notable exception. Though he was perhaps the most accomplished musician of all the reformers, he forbade song in corporate worship in his Reformed Church in Zurich. He believed Scripture did not command it and that music was for secular outward enjoyment rather than inward piety. His worldview was dualistic as we will also see in Chapter Two of this book. See Paul Westermeyer, *Te Deum: The Church and Music,* p. 149-153.

baptism. Zwingli cruelly oversaw the martyrdom of Anabaptists in Zurich. Baptism and animosity aside, however, both traditions had a similar approach to corporate worship. Both denied Christ's *real presence* in Communion and held to a memorialist view. (We will discuss this issue in Chapter Two.) They observed the Table infrequently rather than each week.[17] Both Anabaptists and the Reformed Church insisted on preeminence of the Word in worship.

There were differences, of course. The Anabaptists were social and political pariahs. They denied the efficacy of infant baptism which was not only a spiritual act, but an important rite of citizenship. Anabaptists raised the level of importance for lay leadership and eliminated clergy hierarchy. They kept a low profile, often worshipping in homes to avoid persecution. Anabaptist caution for practical reasons also reinforced their desire to restore the Church to its original New Testament state. The Reformed Church, on the other hand, was fully aligned with and backed by the civic power of the Swiss city-states. They inherited the cathedrals which they stripped of all Catholic adornment in favor of a simple space and liturgy that supported the preaching of the Word.

The Christian family tree spans over two millennia. When we open the picture albums from our earliest years, the images sometimes seem foreign or badly faded. But in the process of dusting them off, we find that we are, indeed, indebted to them. We can see the family resemblance and better understand who we are intended to be. We are inspired by the courage, creativity, passion, and faithfulness of these godly men and women but also warned by the dangers of accommodation to culture and institutionalization. We are encouraged in knowing that God will see to it that his enterprise will always prevail by raising up prophetic and creative renewalists who will "right the ship" when opposition from without and corruption from within threaten to founder the Church. Tracing our ancestral roots deep in the

---

[17] Calvin embraced a mystical view of *real presence* and desired a weekly observance of the Table. But Zwingli's influence came first and was too powerful for Calvin to change in this matter.

archives of Church history is a worthwhile endeavor that would be beneficial for Evangelicals to recover in the local church.

Those who have come before us have shaped us for better or for ill. In this brief overview of the Church's first fifteen hundred years, we have observed significant people and movements which have contributed positively to the Christian Story. Others have presented challenges that have needed to be addressed and corrected. That is how it will always be. The Church may struggle for a season, but it will always overcome its challenges through the gift of people and movements that Christ sovereignly provides to purify his Bride. What follows, then, is a closer look at people and movements which have specifically impacted Evangelicals in the last five hundred years. It is my hope that these portraits will inform, correct, and inspire modern Evangelicals to consider how we might worship God in light of how we have been formed.

Questions for Reflection:

1. Using the metaphor of "ballast" that was presented at the beginning of this chapter, how much "historical ballast" do you have in your personal understanding of the Christian Faith?

2. What difference would "historical ballast" have in the life of your congregation?

3. Of the portraits presented in this chapter, which are most familiar to you? Which of the portraits impact you the most?

4. Do you think Evangelicals need a new "Reformation" in our corporate worship? Why or why not? If so, what do you think needs to be reformed?

Suggested Reading:

Gonzalez, Justo L. *The Story of Christianity, Vol. I: The Early Church to the Dawn of the Reformation,* (New York: Harper Collins Publishers, 2010).

Hall, Christopher A., *Worshipping with the Church Fathers,* (Downers Grove, IL: Intervarsity Press, 2009).

Schaff, Philip and David S., *History of the Christian Church, Vols. I-VI,* (Peabody, MA: Hendrickson Publishers, Marketing, LLC, 1882-1910, Fourth printing, 2011).

Webber, Robert E. ed., *The Complete Library of Christian Worship, Vol. II: Twenty Centuries of Christian Worship,* (Peabody, MA: Hendrickson Publishers, 1994).

Westermeyer, Paul, *Te Deum: The Church and Music,* (Minneapolis: Fortress Press, 1998).

White, James F. *Protestant Worship: Traditions in Transition,* (Louisville, KY: Westminster John Knox Press, 1989).

Trouble at the Table

Here, O my Lord, I see Thee face to face,
Here would I touch and handle things unseen;
Here grasp with firmer hand eternal grace,
And all my weariness upon Thee lean.

Here would I feed upon the bread of God,
Here drink with Thee the royal wine of heaven;
Here would I lay aside each earthly load,
Here taste afresh the calm of sin forgiven.

Horatio Bonar, 1808-1889

Movements in history do not last indefinitely. The energy and enthusiasm from the early days of change wane over time. Reforms can lose their freshness as they are institutionalized by social groups that emerge from the movement. Coupled with the threat of institutionalization, competing interests from the old order subvert or even attack efforts to spread the influence of new ideas.

It was a revived Catholic counter-punch to the Protestant Reformation that led Prince Philip of Hesse to call for a "meeting of the minds" between Martin Luther and Ulrich Zwingli in the fall of 1529. The movement that exploded from Luther's indictment of Rome through his ninety-five theses in 1517 had spread throughout much of central Europe. In Switzerland, Zwingli and other like-minded reformers recruited civic authority to institute even more radical changes than Luther had done in Germany. The Catholic Emperor, Charles V, however, did not cease in his attempts to turn the Reformation back. Fortunately for the new movement, he had his hands full battling Turks who were constantly harassing him on the eastern border of his empire.

But by March, 1529 the Emperor felt that he could turn his attention more fully to religious matters. At the Diet of Speyer, he revoked earlier concessions that he had made to the reformers. The Reformation was now facing stronger resistance than it previously experienced. Prince Philip's call to Luther and Zwingli was an effort to mend cracks in the Reformation edifice that had begun to surface, especially in their understanding of the Lord's Table.

Even prior to their meeting at the Marburg Colloquy, Luther and Zwingli had exchanged several letters explaining their understanding of the Lord's Table. From the outset, finding consensus on the issue with two such polarizing figures as Luther and Zwingli would be a nearly hopeless task. In his letters, Zwingli was complimentary to his protagonist but firm in his position. For his part, Luther called Zwingli a "devil." Philip was fully aware of the struggle ahead of him and invited more moderate voices on both sides to help mediate the process. Luther's ally was Melanchthon; Zwingli's, Oecolampadius. Martin Bucer, it seems, could see both sides.

The Prince was shrewd in his arrangements. He was eager, perhaps even desperate, to bring the two great reformers together to resolve their differences. Although Luther and Zwingli took rooms in the castle at Marburg, they would not actually meet each other until three days after they had arrived. Philip arranged for Luther, Oecolampadius, Zwingli, and Melanchthon to dine together and engage in cordial discussion. Each side had the opportunity to size each other up before the debate would actually begin. These initial theological discussions were friendly, but inconsequential. The die was already cast.

The Marburg Colloquy began officially the morning of October 2, 1529. Luther and Melanchthon were seated on one side of the table, Zwingli and Oecolampadius on the other. Before the debate began, Luther lifted the tablecloth and drew his "line in the sand" with chalk, writing *hoc est corpus meum* ("this is my body") on the table. Luther complained that he had been reluctant to attend the debate. He felt that his writings were clear enough. He then opened fire with criticism of Zwingli's "naturalist" approach to the issue. Christ's words at the Last

Supper must be understood exactly as he said them. "God can do far more than our thoughts suggest," Luther asserted. The Christian should adore the words of God with amazement. Oecolampadius countered that Christ's words regarding the elements at the table were not literal, but metaphorical. The essential point was the meaning of "is" in Christ's words "this *is* my body." Luther countered that his opponent's hermeneutic must be proven. In his mind, nothing in Christ's words demonstrated the necessity of employing metaphor. Oecolampadius invoked "spiritual eating" in John 6:63, the hinge-point of Zwingli's argument, "It is the Spirit that gives life; the flesh profits nothing." Zwingli struck even harder, inferring that Luther had the same attitude as that of a heretic. It was retaliation toward the German who had essentially called him the same thing in the letters they had exchanged.

The debate was stale-mated and the heat was rising.[1]

Exasperated, Luther declared to his opponent, "Your arguments are weak; abandon them and give glory to God."

Zwingli countered, "We too, ask you to do the same thing; we ask you to give glory to God and to abandon your begging of the question…You are twisting the argument. I shall not allow myself to be turned aside. I remain firm at this place, John 6, verse 63. I shall oblige you to return to it. You will have to sing a different tune with me."

Luther invoked faith and the necessity of sustaining mystery at the Lord's Table. Zwingli pressed his exegetical arguments.

Regarding Zwingli's key verse, Luther brushed it aside, "The text has nothing to do with the matter under discussion."

Zwingli shot back, protecting his ground, "No, no, this text will break your spine!"

Luther cut deep, "Do not boast too much. Here necks are not broken. You are in Hesse now, not Switzerland," in reference to the cruel treatment of Anabaptists by the Swiss.

In the end, the two great reformers could not reach agreement on the issue of the nature of the bread and wine at the Lord's

---

[1] The dialogue that follows is from Jean Riliet, *Zwingli: Third Man of the Reformation*, (Philadelphia: Westminster Press, 1964) p. 260.

Table. Curiously, Melanchthon remained essentially silent throughout the debate which dragged on for another day. Both Luther and Zwingli ended their dialogue with mutual compliments for each other, though defiant in the security of their theological positions. Prince Philip of Hesse was anxious for a statement of unity and urged the reformers to declare points on which they were in agreement. The document that they produced was to become known as the Articles of Marburg.

Given the highly contentious nature of the colloquy, the Articles were effective in staking out common theological ground for the Reformation, much to the disappointment of their Catholic opponents. Luther and Zwingli even found agreement on some points regarding the Lord's Table. They repudiated the Catholic Mass as a sacrifice. Zwingli agreed with Luther that the rite was instituted by Christ as a sacrament. Finally, both affirmed the necessity of "spiritual participation in the body and blood of Christ" for every Christian.

Manifestations of Zwingli's Influence

The Protestant Reformation inherited the polarity of thought regarding the Lord's Table represented by Luther and Zwingli. The Anglicans and their heirs generally joined with the Lutherans in embracing "the real presence" of Christ in the bread and wine. Zwingli's influence was widespread throughout the Reformed Church and the theological streams that would follow in their wake. Ironically, Zwingli's view of the Lord's Table was similar to the Anabaptists, many of whom were martyred with his approval. Generally, church traditions that observe the Lord's Table each week hold to a view of "real presence" – that is, Christ is physically present in the bread and the cup. Churches that observe the rite monthly or less frequently typically understand the bread and cup as "representing" Christ's body and blood.

As a life-long Baptist, I grew up in the latter tradition. In my personal journey as a worshipper and worship pastor, I have become impassioned to discover a deeper meaning and observance of the Lord's Table. My hunger for understanding began with a desire for greater personal enrichment. But even more, I have become increasingly aware of impoverishment in my own tradition and seek to lead those whom I shepherd into deeper insight and experience at the Lord's Table.

There is no question that people who have been formed in Zwingli's memorialist view of Communion believe that something uniquely spiritual is transpiring at the Table. We have always approached the rite with the utmost reverence. In fact, the first time that I ever experienced Communion in an Episcopal church, I was offended by their joy. The participants processed in an orderly fashion to the kneeling rails at the altar. Those who served the elements approached the worshippers with a smile and bright countenance. After the people received the elements, they proceeded back to their pews, light on their feet and with a radiance of joy that I had never witnessed in a Communion service. My paradigms were rocked! Something was seriously wrong with those people. After all, remembering Christ's death was a very sobering and serious matter.

Looking back, I am not surprised at my reaction. For most of my Christian life, I approached the Lord's Table in a state of deep contrition for my sins and unworthiness. As I examined myself according to the Apostle Paul's admonition in I Corinthians 11:28, I mentally beat myself up for what I did to Jesus. I was grateful, but more often than not, it was the feeling of guilt that dominated my soul at the Table. Throughout most of my career as a church musician and worship planner, I played or sang songs such as Isaac Watts' classic hymn (which I love) to inspire the same affect in others:

Alas! and did my Savior bleed,
And did my Sovereign die?
Would he devote that sacred head
For sinners such as I?

It was, in effect, what some have crassly referred to as a "funeral service for Jesus." From my vantage point now, I am quite certain that is not at all what Christ intended for the meal.

It seems, unfortunately, that most non-liturgical Evangelicals have a deep aversion to Catholicism, and vice versa. I attended fundamentalist churches in my childhood. I couldn't imagine in my ignorance that Catholics could be truly Christian. Their faith, it seemed to me, was institutional rather than personal. When I moved to a city in the Midwest where Catholicism was the dominant religious influence, the suspicions ran even deeper. Our Baptist congregation sought to drop the denominational label so as to avoid putting off potential ex-Catholics who might want to join our church. In typical Baptist fashion, however, we couldn't agree on a new name so we kept our label. But the anti-Catholic aversion became even more manifest when I attempted to introduce traditional liturgical elements into corporate worship. When I first proposed inviting worshippers to the front of the sanctuary to kneel at a long table to receive the bread and the cup, my suggestion was met with great concern. "We shouldn't do that. It's too Catholic." We did "Stations of the Cross" for Good Friday one year with powerful impact. I gained approval for the service only because I labeled it differently. I never even attempted to ask if we could recite creeds. It was important for my Baptist congregation that the lines of distinction between us and Catholics be rigorously maintained.

...it was the feeling of guilt that dominated my soul at the Table.

Anti-Catholic bias has perhaps impoverished us most when we observe Communion. To distinguish our observance from Catholics, I would frequently hear a pastor refer to the elements as "mere symbols" and say "there's no magic here." In fact, I found myself saying similar things when I officiated at the Table. Such language, however, generally belies a weak understanding of a symbol, even for memorialists. More precise language for the belief I held would be to say that the bread and the cup were "props" in mentally recalling the drama of Christ's crucifixion. (But even this notion, I now realize, was not adequate.) A symbol cannot be "mere." Symbols are elements through which humans

43

communicate complex associations and meaning. For example, when a swastika is brandished before our eyes, it becomes a mental and emotional doorway to the terror and horror of the Third Reich. Most people in our culture will conjure up images of the German army, Hitler, and death camps. Symbols are powerful; they do not stand alone. As symbols, the bread and the cup are a doorway to a much deeper reality. (Similarly, Christ's suffering is not simply a drama to be recalled.) The elements that Christ prescribed for us at the Table are neither "props" nor "mere symbols."

In my experience, I have also been saddened by some pastors who feel that the Lord's Table is an intrusion on their preaching time. For them, the whole rite seems to be a bother. I have heard some suggest that it would be better if their congregation would observe quarterly Communion. In those settings, Communion has been done rather quickly and in a perfunctory manner. Any suggestion that the Lord's Table should receive more time and attention is viewed as a threat to preaching time – which, indeed, it is. In the hierarchy of worship values in those settings, preaching is preeminent, music probably second, prayer perhaps third, and the Lord's Table is an occasional imposition.

Even with the impoverished understanding and practice of the Lord's Table that I have noted above, worshippers in the memorialist tradition do understand the rite to be uniquely important. They intuitively know that something very significant happens when we come to Communion. They hold the experience in such high regard that most cannot consider observing it weekly as Catholic, Lutheran, and Anglican traditions do. When I taught undergraduate students, I understood that my mission was to inspire them as worship renewalists. On occasion, I would challenge them to consider weekly observance of the Lord's Table. The great majority of them rejected the idea. In their minds, the frequency of observance would dilute the impact of the experience. Ironically, virtually all of them subscribed to the value of *daily* devotions.

"Real Presence"
Various Views on the Nature of the Bread and the Cup

Catholic "transubstantiation": The bread and wine become Christ's physical body and blood when the priest says the words of institution, "This is my body."

Lutheran "consubstantiation": Christ's body is "in, with, and under" the bread and the wine. The elements retain their essential substance while simultaneously carrying the body and the blood of Christ.

Calvinist mystery: The Holy Spirit imbues the bread and the wine with the reality of Christ's risen presence when received in faith.

Zwinglian memorialist: Christ is not present in the elements. They are symbols through which the worshipper recalls the saving work of Christ.

Zwingli Reconsidered

It would be a mistake to consider my experience as normative for all traditions that hold to a Zwinglian understanding of the Lord's

Table. Nevertheless, most readers who hold a memorialist view will probably resonate with some of my story. Zwingli himself, however, would probably be dismayed at some of the thought and practice that developed from the position that he staked out at Marburg.

The Reformation was a needed reaction against Catholic religion that had run amok. Prior to that, the Mass had become largely a public performance done by the priest in front of the people. The priest performed the rite with his back to the congregation, often mumbling the Latin liturgy which most of the illiterate worshippers could neither hear nor understand. The cup had long been removed from the people in fear that "Christ's blood" might be inadvertently spilled as a great sacrilege. Since Catholic dogma declared that the bread became Christ's literal body after the words of institution were said, even the sight of the consecrated element became a moment of adoration as it was lifted up before the people. The Mass had become a literal "re-sacrifice" of Christ's body and blood. All Protestant reformers were in agreement that the Catholic rite had gone too far.

Zwingli was influenced by humanism, especially through his contemporary, Erasmus, whom he greatly admired. Erasmus translated the Greek New Testament and was a reformer in his own right, though his efforts remained within the Catholic Church. Through his humanistic influence, Zwingli came to value the Church Fathers and biblical exposition. Unlike Erasmus, however, Zwingli was also influenced by contemporary scholasticism with its emphasis on reason. It was Zwingli's tilt towards reason, as opposed to Luther's appreciation of mystery, that was at the core of their disagreement at Marburg. He questioned how Christ could be physically present in the elements since he had ascended and was seated at the right hand of the Father. Luther maintained the ubiquity of Christ's presence; his body is resurrected, and as a divine person, he can be present in more than one place at a time. Zwingli's foundation of biblical exposition was the reason for his confidence that his key text, John 6:63, would "break the spine" of Luther in their debate.

The Swiss reformer's understanding of the Lord's Table was that it is a memorial of Christ's death. He understood it as a true symbol – a doorway to genuine spiritual experience. At the same time, he denied that the elements were in anyway transformed through the rite. They always remained simply bread and wine. In partaking of the elements, the worshiper honored the atoning work of Christ at the cross. Most likely from his military experience where allegiance is essential, he viewed Communion as a pledge to Christ. Zwingli also rightly recognized St. Paul's emphasis on Christian community (I Cor. 11:17-34) in sharing the meal.

As a humanist and a literal "Renaissance man," Zwingli was influenced by the growing intellectual tides of his time. His theology of the Lord's Table promoted a dualistic conception of things. His insistence on the separation of "spirit and flesh," as he understood John 6:63, lies at the core of his belief. From this theological foundation, Zwingli could not see how any physical thing such as bread or wine could have spiritual benefit in itself. The hard distinction that he made between flesh and spirit would become magnified a hundred years later in the Enlightenment with its clear separation between sacred and secular. This dualistic tendency, which is not found in Hebrew or New Testament thought, would have a growing and unfortunate impact on Western Christianity.

In most of Zwingli's writing concerning the Lord's Table, he insists that the rite offers no opportunity for strengthening the worshipper's faith. It is not surprising, then, that he directed Communion to be observed only quarterly in his church. In truth, his rhythm for observance was essentially the same or better than Catholic practice of the day, since most worshippers had very limited access to the Table. In his later writing, however, Zwingli reversed his understanding and agreed with Luther in a limited sense by affirming that the Lord's Table did indeed strengthen the believer's faith. Zwingli died an untimely death on the battlefield in 1531. We can only speculate about how his theology of the Lord's Table could have continued to evolve. John Calvin, who took up the mantle of leadership in the Swiss Reformed Church, tried to change Zwingli's prescription from quarterly to weekly observance of the Lord's Table but he was unsuccessful. Calvin's nuanced view of the Table was more mystical than Zwingli's and allowed for Christ's presence in the elements through the Holy Spirit when received by faith. Though Calvin would become the dominant theologian in the Reformed tradition, it was Zwingli's memorialist conception of the Lord's Table that would persist as the accepted view.

What Have We Lost at the Table?

My critical view of Ulrich Zwingli has softened over time. In my journey regarding the Lord's Table, I had considered him a villain of sorts, the primary culprit responsible for my impoverished conception of Communion. In truth, my view is still probably more Zwinglian than Lutheran. But within the memorialist view, where the elements remain simply bread and wine, there is a pressing need for renewal in order to recapture what we lost in the polarized debate of the Reformation.

The corporate emphasis of the Lord's Table found in I Corinthians 11 and strongly affirmed in Zwingli's teaching is frequently missing in the practice of non-liturgical churches. I had always been taught and assumed that the purpose of examining oneself prior to Communion, as Paul urged (I Cor. 11:27-30), was to confess the sins that we had committed prior to partaking of the elements. Indeed, I asserted as much in a theological paper that I submitted while I was in school. The professor's comment, "Oh, really?" sent me back to the biblical source.

The central question in self-examination is what it means to partake of the bread and cup "in an unworthy manner." Several commentaries on the passage reflect the same idea that I had been taught, that of testing one's heart attitude regarding our relationship with Christ and an attentive approach to the Table. We should not come in a cavalier manner. Certainly, the nature of the rite demands our care. Reverence may be implied in the passage, but Paul's concern was primarily focused on the dysfunction of the community. The larger context of the passage, including the whole intent of the epistle, was to correct the division that was present in the gifted but immature church. That lack of unity and concern for others manifested itself when worshippers came to the Lord's Table. The apostle excoriates the gluttony and hoarding of food by those who are wealthy because they excluded those who could bring nothing to the meal. His language is strong: "What? Is it really true! Don't you have your own homes for eating and drinking? Or do you really want to disgrace the church of God and shame the poor?" (v. 22a, NLT). Paul's reference to "honoring the body of Christ" (v. 29) is first a reference to life together. The entirety of the next chapter in the epistle is devoted to clarifying the meaning of that metaphor.

The experience of many in non-liturgical traditions like mine is intensely personal, even to the exclusion of the community. People protested when I instituted singing of hymns during the distribution of elements at one of the churches I served. For them, singing was a distraction from their personal reflection and self-examination. And they were right in raising that objection, since they understood the rite solely as interaction between the Lord and themselves personally. I brought corporate singing into the rite because it is one way to bring people together in community. But for my protesting individualistic worshippers, it intruded on their private contemplation.

We will never be worthy to come to the Table of the Lord. We approach because Christ has always welcomed sinners. We come at his invitation. Paul's emphasis, however, is that we need to examine ourselves to see if we are truly acting in love towards our brothers and sisters in Christ. It is no coincidence that Paul elevates love above all Christian gifts and virtues in the context of his instructions on the Table (I Cor. 13). Theologian Wolfhart Pannenberg explains the Apostle's emphasis:

When Paul *warned* against unworthy communion (I Cor. 11:27ff.) he was not concerned with the intrinsic moral condition of the individuals and with a corresponding need for confession and absolution prior to Holy Communion, but rather with a lack of appreciation for the communal implications in the celebration of the Eucharist. Forgiveness of sins is exhibited in the Eucharist itself. Therefore, it obscures the meaning of the Eucharist to make absolution a prior condition for participation. One should be concerned with the social obligations following that participation.[2]

If we truly understood and practiced Paul's teaching, I wonder whether we would not have more peace within our churches. "Forgive us our debts, as we also have forgiven our debtors" (Matt. 6:12). The sobering words of the Lord's Prayer bring the Apostle's teaching into clear focus.

Probably the greatest loss that developed through Zwingli's memorialist approach is that our focus at the Lord's Table can be too limited. The Reformer conceptualized the rite as a memorial of the Lord's death. In practice, memorialists focus their meditation on Christ's crucifixion during Communion. Certainly, Christ's death is the hinge point. But such an approach diminishes the full meaning of the Table. Biblical scholars debate whether or not the meal that Christ shared with his disciples and during which he instituted the Lord's Table was the Passover meal. Whether it was an actual Seder meal is not critical. As Christ superseded the Temple and the Torah, so he also intended the meal that he ordained with his disciples to be the New Passover. Paul identified Christ himself as our Passover (I Cor. 5:7) and the early Christians demonstrated the same understanding through their practice.

> *When we understand the Lord's Table as our Christian Passover, its meaning is not limited just to Christ's death; it is the whole Christ Event...*

When we recognize the Lord's Table as our Christian Passover, its meaning is not limited just to Christ's death; it is the whole Christ Event – his incarnation, ministry, death, resurrection, and ascension – that we celebrate. It is not just his death that has freed

---

[2] Wolfhart Pannenberg, *Christian Spirituality*, (Philadelphia: The Westminster Press, 1983), p. 41.

us from the bondage of sin and death (just as the Exodus freed the Israelites from bondage in Egypt and implanted a national identity within them) but rather the entirety of Christ's work.

This Pascal conception of the Lord's Table opens other doors for our understanding and observance. The heat of the debate at Marburg over the substance of the elements was shocking. In the years that have followed, the intensity of disagreement between streams of Protestantism and the Roman Catholic Church has not waned. The tragedy is that the focus of the debate is misplaced. James F. White, former professor of liturgy at Notre Dame, points out in referring to the Reformers that:

> …they found it hard to think of the Eucharist in other than spatial terms. Christ's presence had to be localized somewhere, whether in heaven or on the altar, since to them the term "substance" had a spatial meaning. Although Luther was most captive to this form of thinking, it also affected the other 16th Century Reformers; instead of seeing the Eucharist as a *time* mystery, they treated it as a *space* mystery, and probed the static problem of locating the body of Christ rather than the dynamic one of making contact with a saving event.[3]

In White's words, the Lord's Table is a "mystery of time" in which we make "contact with a saving event." What he is referring to is a much deeper meaning of remembrance than a mere intellectual recollection of a historical happening. The concept of remembrance that Jesus intended was the same concept that the ancient Hebrews employed when they observed the Passover meal. God instituted the feast through Moses so that his people would always remember and identify with their redemption from slavery out of Egypt. The Exodus was the defining event for Israel. The feast was to be observed by all generations of Israelites in perpetuity. Partaking of the Passover was a mystery of *time*. Each year, as Israel observed the feast, they experienced their redemption anew. They were not transported

---

[3] James F. White, "Where the Reformation Was Wrong on Worship" in *Christian Century*, October 27, 1982. < http://www.religion-online.org/showarticle.asp?title=1348> Accessed February 18, 2011.

back in time, as it were, but rather the Exodus Event itself was brought *forward* to the present.

The New Testament word for remembrance during Communion is *anamnesis*. It bears the same meaning of carrying an event forward into the present. Just as the Hebrews understand their participation in the Exodus Event throughout all generations, so the Christ Event is brought forward into our present for our participation each time we observe the Lord's Table. Ralph P. Martin explains it this way:

> To recall, in biblical thought, means to transport an action which is buried in the past in such a way that its original potency and vitality are not lost, but are carried over into the present. "In remembrance of me," then, is no bare historical reflection upon the Cross, but a recalling of the crucified and living Christ in such a way that He is personally present in all the fullness and reality of His saving power, and is appropriated by the believer's faith.[4]

Understanding participation at the Lord's Table as the Christian Passover opens new doors of spiritual insight. Communion celebrates our participation with Christ in all the fullness of the Christ Event. Our union with Christ is most powerfully symbolized through baptism. But it is also celebrated at the Table when we properly understand the concept of biblical remembrance. The theme of our union with Christ runs throughout the Pauline epistles. We have died and risen with Christ.

Celebrating our union with a crucified, risen, and ascended Christ at Communion, rather than focusing on penitence and reflection limited to the Crucifixion, would be a helpful and significant paradigm shift for most memorialists. My growing understanding of this concept has made a significant difference in my own life, especially after I leave the Table. It is not so much what I bring to the Table as I approach it (sorrow and a deep sense

---

[4] Ralph P. Martin, *Worship in the Early Church,* (Grand Rapids: William B. Eerdmans Publishing Company, 1964) p. 126.

of unworthiness), but rather the encouragement and strengthening that I receive after I have left. I am reminded that I am joined to Christ. I am no longer a slave to sin, but have died to it with Christ (Rom. 6:6-7). Moreover, I have been raised up with him (Col. 3:1) and I am seated with him in the heavenly realms (Eph. 2:6). It is this union with Christ that Lutherans and Catholics celebrate at Communion. For the most part, this vital understanding was lost in my memorialist tradition. But it can and should be recovered when the Lord's Table is conceived as the Christian Passover.

Zwingli's dualism, from his reading of John 6:63, has already been noted. The separation of spirit and flesh has been an unfortunate characteristic of memorialist conception and practice. In my tradition, the word "sacrament" was avoided in deference to the term "ordinance." The emphasis on Christ's institution of the rite, rather than his presence at the Table, produced a quasi-gnostic approach to not only the Table, but also to life itself. Through Zwinglian dualism, we lost the meaning of sacrament. Simply understood, a sacrament is a "physical means of grace." Memorialists would do well to dispel their fear of sacraments and recapture that understanding. We can do so without embracing "real presence" at the Table as Lutheran and Catholic traditions do. We cannot earn eternal life through human effort; Zwingli's key verse affirms that. But the physical realm does matter. Christ himself is the definitive sacrament. The Word became flesh. He is the *ultimte* "physical means of grace."

Opening the door to a sacramental understanding of life fuses spiritual and physical realms together. Indeed, life becomes holistic. Christ is not only present and active at the Table (through *anamnesis*) but also in baptism, Christian marriage, and a healing touch. All of life becomes a place where Christ may be present through the Holy Spirit. All our endeavors may then be avenues through which we pour out our lives, in the words of Harold Best, as "unceasing worship."[5] Understanding all of our life as a potential sacrament would have a deeply formative impact on us.

---

[5] Harold M. Best, *Unceasing Worship,* (Downers Grove, Ill: Intervarsity Press, 2003), p. 18.

Summary and Path for Renewal

The great Reformers, Martin Luther and Ulrich Zwingli, debated at the Marburg Colloquy in 1529 whether or not Christ was physically present in the Communion bread and cup. While they came to agreement on many doctrinal points critical to the Reformation, they split fiercely on the question of "real presence." Zwingli's memorialist position which did not allow Christ's physical presence in the elements would become the dominant view through the Reformed Church and all of its ecclesiastical heirs. Most churches that observe Communion monthly or less frequently share Zwingli's conception of the Lord's Table.

The memorialist position, however, has become impoverished over time. We have lost the emphasis that the Lord's Table is the Christian Passover, and with that loss, the concept that the rite celebrates the fullness of the Christ Event. In addition, our observance of Communion has become primarily personal, losing the Pauline emphasis of a community acting in love towards one another. Finally, Zwingli's dualism cultivated our aversion to a sacramental conception of the Table and to all of life.

Those who hold to a memorialist conception of Communion, however, can recapture the power and meaning of the rite without embracing "real presence":

- Understand the Lord's Table as participation in the fullness of the Christ Event rather than a penitential reflection limited to the crucifixion.
- Embrace and focus on the community experience and expectation of acting in love toward one another.
- Embrace a sacramental understanding of the Table and all of life.
- Devote time and intention to Communion when it is observed. Consider all that it represents and demands of us. This may require rethinking the preeminence of the sermon on Sundays when the rite is observed.

Every family has their "characters" – the strange uncle or the eccentric grandmother – in their family line. The Church has their fair share, too, and Luther and Zwingli rank among some of the most "colorful" characters in our family. An honest look at history shows that both were deeply flawed,[6] but both men were also deeply committed to God's calling in their life and they played a strategic role in the Reformation. Like all families, the Church has its share of dysfunction. It is tragic to look through personal family pictures and note relatives who lost their way or, for some reason, are not reconciled to siblings or parents and no longer have any kind of relationship. It is tragic, too, that the Table that should unite us deeply divides us. I am under no illusion that sacramentalists and memorialists will ever fully agree on the meaning of the bread and the cup. But with deeper reflection on the New Testament's teaching along with consideration of what transpired in the aftermath of the Protestant Reformation, it is my hope that greater understanding of each other and what we do at the Table will enrich our corporate worship and spiritual formation.

In my theological journey, I have moved from being a memorialist to a sacramentalist while still retaining my Zwinglian conception of the elements. Although I still remain a Baptist, I am no longer offended by those joyous Episcopalians coming back from the Communion altar. In fact, I now share their joy.

Questions for Reflection
1. What do you believe happens during Communion?

2. Does your church have a well-formed understanding of Communion? Do you give it adequate consideration and time in your corporate worship?

---

[6] Both men were aggressive personalities. Zwingli was responsible for the martyrdom of Anabaptists in Zurich. He forbade music in corporate worship (especially problematic for a vocational church musician like me). He was also a soldier and died on the battlefield defending his cause. Luther's foibles are well-known: his acerbic wit, his quick temper, his anti-Semitic views, his melancholic and depressive psyche, and he even suggested polygamy as a solution to Prince Phillip's marital problems.

3. How often does your church observe Communion? Why?

4. Does your church perceive a relationship between the Jewish Passover and the Lord's Table? Does the concept of *anamnesis* – where the past becomes the present – inform your understanding of the rite?

5. What mode of receiving the elements (passing them to the seated congregation or processing to a kneeling rail) do you believe is most meaningful and effective?

6. How do you feel about congregational singing during the distribution of the elements?

Suggested Reading

Davis, John Jefferson, *Worship and the Reality of God: An Evangelical Theology of Real Presence* (Downers Grove: Intervarsity Press, 2010).

Martin, Ralph P., *Worship in the Early Church,* (Grand Rapids: William B. Eerdmans Publishing Co, 1974).

Pannenberg, Wolfhart, *Christian Spirituality,* (Philadelphia: Westminster Press, 1983).

Scandrett, Joel, "Reclaiming Eucharistic Piety" in *Ancient and Postmodern Christianity: Essays in Honor of Thomas C. Oden,* (Downers Grove: Intervarsity Press, 2002).

Schmemann, Alexander, *The Eucharist,* (Crestwood, NY: St. Vladimir's Seminary Press, 2003).

Stookey, Laurence Hull, *Eucharist: Christ's Feast With the Church,* (Nashville: Abingdon Press, 1993).

Wallace, Ronald L., *Calvin's Doctrine of The Word and Sacrament,* (Tyler, TX: Geneva Divinity School Press, 1982).

Welker, Michael, *What Happens in Holy Communion?* (Grand Rapids: William B. Eerdmans Publishing Co., 2000).

The Place of Personal Piety

Ah, holy Jesus, how hast thou offended,
that we to judge thee have in hate pretended?

By foes derided, by thine own rejected,
O most afflicted!

Who was the guilty? Who brought this upon thee?
Alas, my treason, Jesus, hath undone thee!
'Twas I, Lord Jesus, I it was denied thee;
I crucified thee.

For me, kind Jesus, was thy incarnation,
thy mortal sorrow, and thy life's oblation;
thy death of anguish and thy bitter passion,
for my salvation.

Therefore, kind Jesus, since I cannot pay thee,
I do adore thee, and will ever pray thee,
think on thy pity and thy love unswerving,
not my deserving.

Johann Heermann, 1585-1647

Ask virtually any evangelical Christian, "What is the single most important question in life?" and the response will likely be, "Do you have a personal relationship with Jesus Christ?" Most of our ministries are designed in some way to pose that question and cultivate a personal response from the people we serve. Many Evangelicals have conversion stories that include strong "before and after" descriptions. Some even expect that such a narrative should be normative for all Christians.

The Watergate cover-up conspiracy of the early 1970's may have brought down an American president but it also formed a backdrop for the conversion of Chuck Colson, who was one of Evangelicalism's most respected leaders in the twentieth century. Colson, a retired Marine officer, was President Nixon's "hatchet man." He was a master of dirty tricks targeting the administration's political enemies. His involvement in Watergate plunged him into a personal crisis which became a catalyst for his conversion to Christianity. The press mocked his new-found faith as a ploy for sympathy and leniency for his misdeeds. But after thirty-five years of radical personal change and tireless service through Prison Fellowship, the ministry he founded, Colson's life demonstrated the transformational power of the "born-again" experience.[1]

Prior to the Reformation, the Church rarely used the term, "born again." For Catholic and Orthodox theologians, regeneration happens at baptism. But for the modern Evangelical, being born again is a cognizant experience that is essential for salvation. Everyone must personally and willingly respond to the gospel. The necessity of having and nurturing a personal relationship with Christ drives virtually all that we do. The imperative of personal conversion is the reason we are so passionate about missions, both locally and around the world. Evangelicals emphasize holiness, discipline, and good works as evidence of a personal relationship with Christ. We affirm the Bible as God's Word and as his revelation of the salvation which can only be found through Jesus Christ. Our commitment to Scripture places a high value on personal reading and devotion, Bible-centered preaching, and the establishment of societies for the distribution of God's Word.

Because we value a personal relationship with Christ so highly, we tend to be suspicious of the institutional Church with all its historic worship practices, such as set prayers, liturgies, and

---

[1] Colson's testimony is told in his first published book, *Born Again*. (Grand Rapids: Chosen Book, 1976).

creeds. Evangelicals tend to resist words being put into our mouths. We like to improvise our own prayers and thoughts as a reflection of the authenticity of our personal faith. That being the case, many Evangelicals might be shocked to learn that the roots of our movement can be traced back to seventeenth-and-eighteenth-century Lutheran Pietism, where the values we hold today were firmly embraced and institutionalized in Halle, Germany.

An Unsung Evangelical Hero

August Hermann Franke (1663-1727) had prepared himself for vocational ministry. Already educated and credentialed as a Lutheran pastor, he sensed that he was missing the mark as a "true Christian." In 1687, he received a new opportunity in Luneburg, Germany, where he would spend his time in private study and fellowship with devout and pious Christians. Shortly after his arrival, he was asked to preach at the local church. He was instructed that the sermon must be directed to the heart and conscience of the hearer. His text was John 20:31: "[These signs]...are written so that you may believe that Jesus is the Christ, the Son of God, and that by believing you may have life in His name." Preparation for the sermon drove him to despair:

> ...as I now pondered this with all seriousness, it came to me that I possessed no such faith as I demanded. I thus came away from meditation on the sermon and found enough to do within myself because such, namely that I still had no true faith, came deeper and deeper into my heart. I wanted to rise immediately and drive these dismal thoughts away, but nothing would suffice. I was until that time, accustomed to relying on my own reason, with good cause because in my heart I had experienced little of the new reality of the Spirit.[2]

---

[2] As quoted in Gary R. Sattler, *God's Glory, Neighbor's Good,* (Chicago: Covenant Press, 1982) 29.

Over the course of several days, Franke's despair and disbelief deepened. In pondering the text, he discovered that he had no real faith; that indeed, he did not even believe in God or his Word. Nevertheless, he persevered in his discipline of prayer and study, not wishing to disappoint those who had asked him to preach. He was in great distress and sorrow with no refuge of genuine faith in a Savior. Like Augustine and Luther before him and countless others who would follow, he was in deep despair for his soul when God finally intervened:

> In such great anxiety I fell again to my knees on that Sunday eve and cried to God – who I neither knew nor believed – for salvation from such a sorrowful condition, if there was truly a God. Then the Lord heard me, the living God from his holy throne, as I was still on my knees....Then, as one turns his hand (in a twinkling), so all my doubts were gone; I was sure in my heart of the grace of God in Jesus Christ; I knew God not only as God, but rather as one called my Father. All sadness and unrest in my heart was taken away in a moment. On the contrary, I was suddenly so overwhelmed as with a stream of joy that I praised out of high spirits that God who had shown me such great grace. I arose again of a completely different mind than when I had knelt down. I had bent down with great sorrow and doubt, but arose again with inexpressible joy and great assurance. As I knelt, I did not believe there was a God. As I arose I would have confirmed it without fear or doubt, even with the shedding of my blood.[3]

Franke was "born again" through the experience which would shape the rest of his life and ministry. The deep wrestling of his soul would become known as *busskampf* or "penitential struggle." While Franke did not prescribe his path as a normative means to be born again, the penitential struggle would become a common theme in conversion narratives for Pietists.[4]

---

[3] *Ibid.,* 31.

[4] Penitential struggle prior to conversion did become the norm in the American First Great Awakening. Jonathan Edwards describes the suffering of those seeking salvation in New England as did David Brainerd in his

August Hermann Franke should be considered second-generation among Lutheran Pietists, but the ministry that he established at Halle was the pinnacle of achievement and influence for the movement. F. Earnest Stoeffler, the father of American Pietism scholarship, said this of him:

> Franke is undoubtedly one of the most massive figures of the late seventeenth and early eighteenth centuries in Europe. As a religious genius he fashioned Spenerian Pietism into one of the most self-assured, theologically compact, as well as dynamic, religious movements of the day.[5]

The Ministry at Halle

The ministry at Halle was wide-ranging. Franke was particularly moved by the plight of the poor while at the same time cultivating relationships with the ruling elite. He became friends with his monarch, Frederick Wilhelm I, even though the king was Reformed. He corresponded with Peter the Great of Russia and the influential English Society for Promoting Christian Knowledge. He had friends in Scandinavia as well as in the American colonies. Franke's political skills enabled him to build the support that he needed to develop his ministry.

Halle had a very active printing enterprise. Between 1712 and 1719, Franke and his enterprise printed 100,000 German Bibles and 80,000 New Testaments. By comparison, it took Wittenberg, the previous leader in publishing the Scriptures, nearly one hundred years to print and distribute that same number. Pietists placed a high value on personal Bible reading. The operation in Halle fulfilled a dream of making the Bible a "book of the people." Franke's business enterprise was not just limited to publishing, however. The ministry was also supported by a thriving fur and wine import business – made all the more profitable by privileges

---

ministry with the Indians. One hundred years later, under Charles Finney's influence, the process of conversion would no longer include the expectation of *busskampf*.

[5] F. Earnest Stoeffler, *German Pietism in the Eighteenth Century*, (Leiden, Netherlands: E.J. Brill, 1973) 36.

that he had negotiated with the monarch. Halle's educational system was comprehensive. In the university, Franke developed a model for training ministers and teachers that would be worthy of emulation today. Along with academic rigor in their studies, his students were expected to apply their knowledge and skills in Halle ministry institutions: orphanages, biblical training for young people (catechism), and schools for all ages and social strata.

Franke also had a heart for world evangelization. Foreign leaders looked to him to help supply missionaries for their colonial interests. When thirty thousand Protestants were driven from the Salzburg region, many of them immigrated to the Georgia Colony in America. Halle provided ministerial and financial support for the refugees. Heinrich Melchior Muhlenberg, who established the first organized Lutheran church in Pennsylvania, was sent and financed by Franke. Halle's influence was far-reaching and profound. Swedish pastors who had been trained there promoted spiritual revival among compatriot prisoners in Siberia who, in turn, would influence their homeland when they were finally released. Franke also had a close and supportive relationship with Count Nicolas Von Zinzendorf, the leader of the Moravians, who were very active in mission work and would eventually play a vital role in the conversions of John and Charles Wesley.

The entrepreneurial accomplishments of August Hermann Franke were extraordinary. But at his core, he was a pastor who had a heart that burned with passion for God and His work. Though politically shrewd, he was uncommonly kind and gentle. His sermons were unremarkable: hastily prepared, repetitive, and lacking in illustration. (Perhaps that is no wonder; he had to prepare and deliver up to five sermons a week along with all of his other duties.) Still, he was a very popular pastor; his sermons were attended by large crowds. He abolished group confession in favor of a private interview with the pastor. Franke insisted that families and the church work together in child-raising, so he reestablished catechism for children and made pastoral visits in homes. He was charming, transparent, and sincere: a model of authentic Christian faith. Prior to his conversion, Franke had sought to become a "true Christian." By all accounts, he did not miss the mark.

Pietist Beginnings

Fifty years prior to Franke's experience at Luneburg, the European continent was in upheaval, embroiled in the Thirty Years War (1618-1648), a struggle for religious domination between Catholic, Reformed, and Lutheran powers. Up to thirty percent of the population was decimated through warfare, famine, and disease. The fight was waged not only on the field, but also in religious debate. Pastors were not trained in exegesis of the Scriptures or in practical theology, but rather in polemics, the art of arguing one's point of view. Such an approach may be understandable when the survival of the church and state was threatened by armies representing competing theological persuasions.

By 1648 when the war was settled by the Peace of Westphalia, the German Lutheran Church was in bad shape. Morale was low, and spirituality, where it existed, was generally sterile and forced. Even the lifestyles of the clergy left much to be desired, with many characterized by arrogance, drunkenness, a worldly spirit, and desire for carnal pleasures. Apparently there was no personal conviction that one's Christian faith should be manifested in behavior. Clearly, the church was in need of renewal.

Philip Jacob Spener (1635-1705) would become the catalyst for needed reform in the German Lutheran Church. As a child, he possessed a fervent faith and an insatiable love of learning. He was influenced by his reading of English Puritan books – devotional works that were critical of conventional Christianity and promoted a heartfelt personal faith with a quest for holy living. Spener prepared himself for a vocation of teaching but never strayed from the Puritan influence. His early adulthood was marked by devotion to his faith and education. After he completed his studies, it was no surprise that he was ordained for ministry.

In 1675, Spener was asked to write the preface for a Lenten issue of sermons on the Gospels by Johann Arndt (1555-1621). Arndt's work was perennially popular and it was his spirit that would inspire the Pietist Movement.[6] A sample of one of his prayers illustrates his devotional fervor:

> My Jesus, Bridegroom of my soul! Come and betroth Thyself to me with grace and mercy, yeah, even in faith! Dwell and abide in me! Draw me unto Thee and into Thee so that Thy will and my will may be one, so that I share the divine nature and so that I may never again be separated from Thy love either in life or in death. Amen.[7]

Spener's preface to Arndt's sermons would become the framework for German Pietism. His essay was immediately embraced by the public and reissued as a separate work. The full title shows Spener's intention: *Heartfelt Desire for a God-Pleasing Reform of the True Evangelical Church, Together with Several Simple Christian Proposals Looking Towards This End.* The author issued the work in German and in Latin. It is known by its shortened title, *Pia Desideria.* Spener criticized social defects in civil authorities, clergy, and the common people. He proposed correctives through more extensive use of Scripture, exercise of the spiritual priesthood of believers, and a practical, lived-out faith rather than one that was merely intellectualized.[8]

Even with all of its good intentions and outcomes, Lutheran Pietism was not without its detractors. The most controversial practice of the Pietists was their home meetings where they regularly met for Bible and devotional reading. These conventicles, as they were called, were viewed with suspicion by the orthodox Lutherans, and with good reason. Although Pietist leaders instructed home group leaders to guard against the inclination to disassociate from the church, they were not always successful. Because of the subjective and individualistic nature of Pietist faith, it has an unfortunate history of breeding separatist

---

[6] Arndt was most well-known for his work, *True Christianity* (1606), which became a classic and favorite reading, second only to the Bible for German Pietists.

[7] John Joseph Stoudt. *Devotions and Prayers of Johann Arndt,* (Grand Rapids, MI: Baker Book House, 1958), 57.

[8] Pietism is often simply described as "religion of the heart."

Pietist Awakenings in the Eighteenth Century

1708 Silesia - *Kinderbeten* (children's prayer meetings) was the spark that ignited a broader awakening throughout the region.

1713 Siberia - Revival among Swedish prisoners would impact their homeland upon their return.

1721 New England - Stirrings of the "First Great Awakening" emerged in the American colonies.

1727 Herrnhut - Revival among the Moravian Brethren immigrants at Zinzendorf's estate.

1730 Salzburg - Revival among Protestant miners who would eventually be exiled by Catholic edict. Many of the refugees immigrated to America.

1736 Northern Germany- Dramatic revival broke out in small villages characterized by weeping and cases of healings.

1738 England – The conversions of John and Charles Wesley were the catalyst for the expansion of street preaching and establishment of Methodist Societies.

1739 New England - George Whitfield's embarked on his second trip to America at the height of the First Great Awakening.

None of these revivals stood alone. These events should be seen as part of a series of awakenings, often inspired by a complex network of relationships among Pietist leaders.

---

groups. Still, to his credit, Spener did not seek to form a new church, though he may have been able to do such a thing, so great was his influence. Unlike their spiritual cousins, the English Puritans, Spenarian Pietists sought and were successful in achieving reform within the Lutheran Church.

The orthodox Lutherans also criticized Pietism as legalistic for the tendency to systematize Christian behavior into acceptable and unacceptable categories. Many Pietist groups prohibited dancing, theatre, and all other worldly diversions. Their aversion to secular entertainment and preference for religious expressions that evoked emotion led them to favor simple music in worship. Like the focus of Franke's sermon, which was influenced by the faithful in Luneburg, Pietist song had to resonate with the heart rather than stimulate the mind.

The Worship Values of Lutheran Pietism

Before Spener sought to renew the Lutheran Church through *Pia Desideria,* German mystics and hymn-writers expressed the fire of devotion in their works. Along with Arndt, the works of Jakob Bohme (1575-1624), with his emphasis on the new birth, would be influential in Pietist thought. Angelus Silesius (1624-1677) was a disciple of Bohme. His hymns were popular with the Pietists and expressed a deep longing and love for God, as in this example translated by John Wesley:

Thee will I love, my Strength, my Tower,
Thee will I love, my Joy, my Crown,
Thee will I love with all my power,
In all thy works, and thee alone;
Thee will I love, till the pure fire
Fill my whole soul with pure desire.[9]

The best-loved Pietist hymn that survives from that era in our contemporary hymnals is "Jesus, Priceless Treasure," by Johann Frank (1618-1677). J.S. Bach used the work as the basis for one of his cantatas. The song's main idea was borrowed from a contemporary secular love song of the period, *Flora, meine Freude.* A literal translation of the text illustrates the heart-felt devotion

[9] Johann Scheffle, John Wesley, tr., *Thee Will I Love, My Strength, My Tower,* http://www.oremus.org/hymnal/t/t411.html. Accessed 2/7/09.

along with the sentimentality that would frequently characterize the genre:

> Jesus, my joy, my heart's longing,
> Jesus, my beauty:
> Oh, how long, how long is the heart's concern
> and longing after you.
> Lamb of God, my bridegroom,
> may nothing on earth be dear to me except you.
> Get out! Spirit of sadness, for my Lord of gladness –
> Jesus enters in.
> To those who love God, even their sorrows are purest sugar.[10]

Pietists were prolific hymn writers. Johann Freylinghausen was Franke's son-in-law and editor of the massive hymnal *Geistreiches Gesang-Buch,* which included over eight hundred hymns in its second edition. There are, however, few that survived the filter of time to be sung today. Most lacked poetic and theological strength. Some hymns, like the following example from the Moravians, were characterized by devotional heat beyond the bounds of propriety and restraint: "He it is who conquers my heart, for he lies between my hot breasts like a sprig of myrrh arousing in me holy lust…"[11] Like the opening line, the rest of the lyric would make even the most jaded person blush.

The seventeenth century has been called the golden age of Lutheran hymnody, even with its excess and sentimentality. The best and most influential hymn writer from the era was Paul Gerhardt (1607-1676). Most hymnals today include his translation of the medieval poem, "O Sacred Head Now Wounded" and perhaps "Jesus, Thy Boundless Love to Me." A comparison of Gerhardt's

---

[10] Donald P. Hustad, *Jubilate II*, (Carol Stream, IL: Hope Publishing Company, 1993) 205.

[11] Hedwig T. Durnbaugh, *The German Hymnody of the Brethren 1720-1903,* (Philadelphia, PA: The Brethren Encyclopedia, Inc., 1986) 30.

The effects of the Thirty Years War were devastating. Martin Rinkart was a pastor in Eilenburg, Saxony during the period. Through starvation, disease, and effects of war, he would bury as many as fifty people a day while the war waged on. His wife was one of the victims. He was instrumental in securing relief from an unreasonable ransom demanded of the poverty-stricken city by the Swedish army. Shortly after the end of the war, he penned this well-known hymn, expressing Pietist faith in the face of overwhelming suffering.

Now thank we all our God, with heart and hands and voices,
Who wondrous things has done, in Whom this world rejoices;
Who from our mothers' arms has blessed us on our way
With countless gifts of love, and still is ours today.

O may this bounteous God through all our life be near us,
With ever joyful hearts and blessèd peace to cheer us;
And keep us in His grace, and guide us when perplexed;
And free us from all ills, in this world and the next!

Martin Rinkart, c. 1636

hymns with Luther's chorales is insightful. Luther's hymns depict God as powerful and gracious; Gerhardt viewed God as gentle and loving. Luther's hymns are more corporate and Gerhardt's more personal, frequently beginning with the personal pronoun, "I." In a sense, his hymns did not proclaim the truth of the gospel; they lived them. Other notable Pietist hymns from the era that appear in modern hymnals include, "Ah, Holy Jesus," "If You Will Only Let God Guide You," and perhaps best-known of all, "Now Thank We All Our God." All express deep personal devotion to Christ, often within the context of suffering.

Pietism gave us a rich deposit of hymns which express personal devotion to Christ. But with this valuable contribution also came the danger to sentimentalize the faith and prescribe a certain worship experience expected of all:

Pietism's danger was to erect a means to reach God with the heart...Where Pietists kept strong preaching traditions, they were able to stay in touch with the church's historic faith. Where they lost [preaching and sacraments], they easily slid into a cultural moment. When Pietists expected everybody to feel the same way, they undermined the church's worship with its freedom and welcome for people of various pieties at different stages or developments in their lives. Musically, they have been prone to trade the bold rejoicing of Luther's chorales for something more intent on creating a response rather than voicing it.[12]

Modern Evangelicals resonate deeply with the Pietist impulse which ran from English Puritanism in the early seventeenth century through German Pietism in the late seventeenth and early eighteenth centuries, all the way through the ministry of John and Charles Wesley. Indeed, the Pietist impulse is the historical taproot of Evangelicalism. In Pietism, we see our core values expressed: the necessity of regeneration, experiential faith, personal Bible reading, study, and devotions, pursuit of personal holiness, service to others, and the imperative of evangelism.

Pietism and the American Spirit

After Franke, Pietism on the European continent began to wane because of flawed leadership, the tendency to separate, and unceasing opposition from orthodox Lutherans. Even the Methodist movement weakened in England after the Wesley era passed. That was not the case, however, in America. Pietism resonated in the spirit of a new nation founded on principles of individualism. Jefferson reasoned individual freedom into the founding documents. Benjamin Franklin, through *Poor Richard's Almanac*, gave voice to the pragmatist, "God helps those that help themselves." Individualist values are embedded into the American soul. Sociologist Robert Bellah observes:

---

[12] Paul Westermeyer, *Te Deum: The Church and Music*, (Minneapolis: Fortress Press, 1998) 230-231.

Individualism lies at the very core of American culture…We believe in the dignity, indeed the sacredness, of the individual. Anything that would violate our right to think for ourselves, judge for ourselves, make our own decisions, live our lives as we see fit, is not only morally wrong, it is sacrilegious. Our highest and noblest aspirations, not only for ourselves, but for those we care about, for our society and for the world, are closely linked to our individualism. Yet…some of our deepest problems both as individuals and as a society are also closely linked to our individualism.[13]

Pietism, in all its forms, found a ready home in America. The cornerstone of our faith, "a personal relationship with Jesus Christ," echoed deeply in the soul of a nation that valued the dignity and choice of an individual. But with the convergence of cultural and religious individualism, American Evangelicals who are deeply rooted in the Pietist tradition have also inherited a number of troubling tendencies that are frequently manifested in our corporate worship. It is time that we faced them.

Individualistic Pietism and Corporate Worship

The American spirit today is obsessed with "me." Self is central. This is obvious to any observer of pop culture or our marketing campaigns. Celebrities go from one relationship to another in order to find happiness and personal fulfillment. We are told over and over by salesmen who do not know us, "you deserve" whatever commodity they are hawking. Nearly fifty years ago, historian Christopher Lasch labeled the contemporary milieu as *The Culture of Narcissism.* Narcissism is an unhealthy obsession with one's self. Though it is considered a psychological abnormality for which there is a clinical diagnosis, Lasch extended his critique to our whole society. He saw the malaise as pervasive in our schools, in sports, in entertainment, in religion, and ultimately in the fear of old age. Our era is an "age of diminishing

---

[13] Robert N. Bellah, et. al., *Habits of the Heart: Individualism and Commitment in American Life,* (New York: Harper and Row, 1985), 32.

expectations." Unlike those who came before us, we live for ourselves rather than our predecessors or our posterity. "People today hunger not for personal salvation, let alone for the restoration of an earlier golden age, but for the feeling, the momentary illusion, of personal well-being, health and psychic security."[14]

Not much has changed in our national psyche of self-obsession since 1979. What Lasch described is essentially accepted as normal now. Worse, cultural narcissism has also made its way into the evangelical church. In the 1980's we began marketing and programming to draw Baby Boomers back to the church as religious consumers. Although Evangelicals have now begun to question the approach to church growth from that era, our practices have deeply formed us, and they have affected the expectations of people in the church. As Lasch suggested, religious seekers are looking not for personal salvation from their sin, but rather for a teaching or experience that will simply make them feel better. The therapeutic impulse in Christian ministry can be heard in the play rotation of most Christian radio stations.[15] Many, if not most, of the songs reflect a theme of personal fulfillment through faith in Christ. Such a theme is not necessarily wrong in itself. It is just that the focus on the individual is so pervasive. In the church, much of our worship has become not so much a celebration of God's mighty acts and our inclusion into his story, but rather an exercise in propping up the worshipper's self-esteem. Don't believe it? Here are some of the things that I have heard and read in a worship setting:

> *...cultural narcissism has also made its way into the evangelical church.*

---

[14] Christopher Lasch, *The Culture of Narcissim: American Life in An Age of Diminishing Expectations,* (New York: W.W. Norton & Company, 1979), 5.

[15] "Positive and Encouraging" is the motto of K-Love, the most widely franchised broadcaster of Christian music in the United States.

"Aren't you glad we have a God who serves us?" This spontaneous comment was spoken by a worship leader in a church that I once attended regularly. I know that Christ came as a servant. But when the comment was made, it was meant to encourage the worshipper's spirit rather than inspire us to service.

"There's a place in God's heart that only you can fill." The author is unknown, but the phrase is quoted throughout the Internet in blogs and sermons. I even heard it used as the basis for teaching by a visiting minister in a seminary chapel who was brought in for a day-long retreat. A needy god isn't the God of the Bible.

"You are the center of God's universe." This heresy was written in a book by a popular former worship leader. I was floored when I read it and still find it hard to believe that respected leaders endorsed the work and Christian editors approved it![16]

A narcissistic and therapeutic approach to worship has become so prevalent in our evangelical services that we often fail to recognize it. People want their preferences honored and are not afraid to complain until they get what they want. (Anyone who has been a worship leader or pastor within the last forty years can readily testify to that!) We have split congregations to form others from the same church in order to satisfy the personal tastes of our people. People want to be emotionally moved. Worshippers demand a sermon that meets their felt-needs and entertains them; and all that we do in corporate worship needs to measure up to the latest Christian music concert, or people will go somewhere

---

[16] Bob Sorge, *Secrets of the Secret Place: Keys to Igniting Your Personal Time with God,* (Kansas City, MO: Oasis House, 2010), 108. I was reluctant to cite the book because I respect and admire the intention of it. Nevertheless, unbridled passion for intimacy with God without good theology can lead to heresy, as illustrated here. Sorge is not alone, however, in his theological misstep. Heresy has happened frequently throughout the history of Christian mysticism. Passionate spirituality must be joined with thoroughly reflective theology, otherwise it becomes self-serving.

else to find what they want. Worshippers want a holy "buzz" or they feel like they have not engaged with God.

Doing Worship as God's Story

Renewalist Robert Webber's diagnosis of our evangelical malaise was that we have placed ourselves at the center of worship. We have become the focus, instead of God. In the years leading up to his death in 2007, Webber was prolific in his writings critical of evangelical narcissism and therapeutic worship. He used a worship song that was popular at the time to illustrate his point:

> Jesus, Lover of my soul, all-consuming fire is in Your gaze.
> Jesus, I want You to know, I will follow You all my days.
> For no one else in history is like You.
> And history itself belongs to You.
> Alpha and Omega, You have loved me,
> And I will share eternity with You.
> It's all about You, Jesus,
> And all this is for You, for Your glory and Your fame.
> It's not about me, as if You should do things my way;
> You alone are God and I surrender to Your ways.[17]

Ironically, the text clearly reflects the opposite idea of any self-focus. Webber's point, however, is that the subject of the song is the singer rather than God. Even though the song says, "It's all about You, Jesus" the action in the song is all from the worshipper, "*I* want you to know...*I* will follow...*I* will share eternity...*" (emphasis mine). It is a good song. I have used it in corporate worship and I would use it again. It is a song of response – and our response is the complement to God's revelation in biblical worship. But Webber's point is insightful. We have made ourselves the central part of worship by making ourselves the subject. The song, although good, is illustrative of our personal focus. Webber's prescription for our problem is to

---

[17] Paul Oakley, *Jesus Lover of My Soul,* © 1995 Thankyou Music (PRS) (Administered by EMI Christian Music Publishing)

make God both the subject and the object of our worship. Worship, as he understands it, is doing God's story:

> Historic worship does this story in its processions into the presence of God, in its praise of God, in its confession of the sins of the world and of self, in its prayers for peace and stability for the peoples of the world, in its Scripture reading and preaching (which tells the story), in its hymns (which sings the story), in the sacraments of baptism (which call us to live in the story), and supremely in the Eucharist (which ushers us into the consummation of the story in the cosmic supper of the Lamb)....Doing the truth of God's story results in the feeling of delight in God, in the formation of personal character, in the emergence of an alternative community, in a reckless abandonment of self to a participation in the life of God in the story of God making us and his world new.[18]

What Webber was describing is a new way for Evangelicals to think about the Church and God's mission in the world and how it is expressed in worship. Making disciples is central to the mission of God, but the mission is about much more than personal salvation. For Webber, historic worship also celebrates God's mission of justice, mercy, and making all things (including the whole cosmos) new through Christ. Conceptualizing worship as doing God's story could have a powerful renewing influence on the whole church.

Utilizing Corporate Expressions

One of the ways in which we can dramatically refocus our worship is to address the pervasiveness of songs that utilize first-person pronouns – "I-me-my songs." The Pietist tradition has given us personal songs of devotion and they are a gift. When Paul Gerhardt asked, "What language shall I borrow to thank Thee, dearest friend?" he gave the worshipper words for authentic and

---

[18] Robert E. Webber, "Is Our Worship Killing Christianity in America?" In *Worship Leader,* November/December, 2005, 10.

passionate personal engagement with the Savior in adoration. Pietists have long criticized – with some merit – Christians outside of our born-again tradition for "going through the motions" of worship without real heart. Pietist song has given the church an avenue to express the reality of personal faith in our worship.

Along with the benefits of personal songs, however, we have also inherited the liabilities of our individualism. Perhaps the songs that most reflect an unhealthy focus are those which express a "romantic" relationship with Christ. These songs are prevalent in today's evangelical culture. In fact, spiritual romance, often equated with *eros,* has long existed in mysticism and Pietism as earlier examples in this chapter have shown. Further, I have found that a romantic orientation to our relationship with Christ is fiercely guarded and defended among many Evangelicals. My attempts to challenge it in my own local church and even in the academy were met with quick objections.

A full critique of spiritual romance or bridal mysticism, as it is called, would require another chapter or book. There are two primary reasons why I believe it is counterproductive to healthy spirituality. First, I believe bridal mysticism is based on a flawed approach to interpreting the Song of Solomon.[19] Origen (c. 185-254 AD) was the first Christian commentator to spiritualize the book. He lived in an era that saw sexuality as evil. He famously castrated himself. Origen and those who followed him did the only thing they could do with the Song – they de-sexed and spiritualized it. Such an approach is not necessary. The Song, as it was intended, offers God's people insight into and celebration of the mystery of human sexuality. The love poem is a wonderful gift if interpreted literally rather than allegorically. It is true that marriage is a picture of God's passion for his people. Paul says so clearly in Ephesians 5:32, and the story of Hosea also powerfully illustrates the idea. But the Bride is always a corporate metaphor, not the individual soul as Origen and most mystics assert.

Second, modern ideas of romance are, by their very nature, self-focused. We "fall in love" to find happiness and our

---

[19] I find the rationale of theologian, Tremper Longman III, to be compelling. *The New International Commentary on the Old Testament: The Song of Songs,* (Grand Rapids, MI: William B. Eerdmans Publishing Company) 2001.

true selves. Such an approach only magnifies a therapeutic and narcissistic approach to worship. Historic bridal mysticism and the modern version differ in one very significant way. The ancients pursued God passionately through self-resignation; moderns seek intimacy with God for self-fulfillment. For this reason, I believe it is best to avoid songs that have romantic allusions in corporate worship.

Along with avoiding romantic worship songs, I have found it very helpful to include more songs with corporate pronouns (we, us, ours) than those that express individual worship. It's not that those songs are wrong. It's that they are so pervasive. But things are changing. Following Webber's lead, theologians and other church leaders have increasingly called attention to narcissism in our evangelical culture, leading some song writers to pen more lyrics with a corporate perspective. That is an encouraging trend.

When I taught worship leadership at Huntington, many of my students were leaders in the campus chapel program. As I articulated these ideas, I noticed that the song selection began to change in the chapels which were designated for extended worship – where the students would sing for forty minutes or more. The balance of song selections moved from predominately individualistic to corporate over time, and I recognized an unforeseen benefit. After the students had sung five to seven songs that brought them together in corporate expression, the few individualistic songs had a freshness and weight which they didn't have when they were the predominant expression. I have found this to be true also in the local church. Using fewer individualistic songs raises the level of their impact!

Using fewer individualistic songs raises the level of their impact!

Getting Over Our Aversion to Set Forms

One of the requirements in a course I taught was for students to attend a worship service from a tradition other than their own and to write a guided reflection paper on their experience. Most of the evangelical students in the class chose to experience a Catholic Mass. Almost without exception, they were awestruck by the beauty of the worship space. Many appreciated the Stations of the Cross that were depicted in pictures or small sculptures around the sanctuary. Their most common criticism – and it was almost universal – was the set liturgy. To my students, it seemed as if many of the worshippers were "mindless robots," moving their lips to the liturgy that they had said over and over, without any passion or real intention from the heart.

People who hold to the Pietist tradition have a deep aversion to set prayers and liturgy. The Puritans, especially, reacted against the liturgy of the Anglican Church. They stripped their worship of all set prayers and what they would consider "high-church" invention and pretense. Cotton Mather, a New England Congregationalist minister, described their manner of worship, "not in any prescribed form of prayer, or studied liturgy, but in such a manner, as the Spirit of grace and of prayer helps our infirmities."[20] He would not allow worshippers to kneel at the Lord's Table because he believed that the action was adoration of the elements – a reaction against the "real-presence" theologies of the Catholic, Lutheran, and Anglican churches.

I was a late-comer to liturgical, "high-church" worship. My roots run deep and wide in the "low-church" tradition. I held all the suspicions and prejudices that a good conservative Baptist would have against liturgical worship. It wasn't until I began to worship twice a year in an evangelical Episcopal church during my pilgrimages to the Robert E. Webber Institute for Worship Studies that I began to see new possibilities. Admittedly, I had my struggles. I especially chafed at the assignment given to my class to craft and lead a service of "baptismal renewal" – a common tradition for those practicing infant baptism. I figured if they had done it right in the first place we wouldn't have to go through all the hassle. I didn't realize how impoverished I was. I had

---

[20] Darrell Todd Maurina, "John Cotton's New England Congregational Model of Worship" in *Twenty Centuries of Christian Worship: The Complete Library of Christian Worship, Vol. II,* Robert E. Webber, ed., (Peabody, MA: Hendrickson Publishers, Inc., 1994), 228.

generally considered Christian baptism (subsequent to conversion in my tradition) simply as a step of obedience and a public declaration of personal faith. I also knew that baptism was the believer's identification with Christ in his death and resurrection. But when I experienced the service of baptismal renewal, I began to understand that baptism is more than a one-time event: it is an experiential reality – daily living and dying with Christ.

While at the Institute, I also began to experience the richness of set prayers and liturgy when enacted with meaning and real heart. As I let down my guard and opened my mind, I began to embrace the richness of an ancient tradition without the threat that, somehow, I was losing my faith. On the contrary, I found that I was enriched. Kneeling at the altar to receive Communion brought a new level of engagement for me as my body expressed what my whole being wanted to do. As I prayed the set prayers in community, I felt a strong sense of solidarity with my fellow worshippers and with those who had prayed the same prayers and made the same confessions hundreds of years before. Utilizing the ancient prayers, confessions, and forms – all with authentic intention from the heart, of course – would be an effective antidote to the problems of individualization that plague so much of evangelical worship. I remember the first time that I confessed with my brothers and sisters the ancient mystery of the faith – "Christ has died; Christ is risen; Christ will come again!" I was part of a much larger story. For me, such experiences were very moving, and I was profoundly shaped by them.

Pietists are right in insisting that our faith and our worship be real and heartfelt. But our aversion to set prayers and liturgy has

Utilizing the ancient prayers, confessions, and forms... would be an effective antidote to the problems of individualization that plague so much of evangelical worship.

impoverished us. We seem to think that if our words are prepared and written for us then our worship is somehow not Spirit-empowered. Certainly, we don't want to express something that has not come from our heart. But the truth is, we sing "prepared worship words" with all of our songs and hymns and yet we believe that our music may be Spirit-empowered. Outside of the church, most American Evangelicals believe we can sincerely recite prepared words in the Pledge of Allegiance to the flag. The fact is we are inconsistent in our rejection of prepared texts for the expression of personal conviction.

We need to rid ourselves of the notion that prepared words cannot be meaningful and sincere. Many of our hymns and songs were put to paper long ago; yet we continue to sing them. Why not consider from time to time including an ancient prayer like the *Te Deum*, reciting a creed on Communion Sunday, or utilizing some of the rich material in the *Book of Common Prayer*? When spoken with real passion and intention, I am certain that our congregations would be enriched.

You are God: we praise you;
You are the Lord; we acclaim you;
You are the eternal Father:
All creation worships you.
To you all angels, all the powers of heaven,
Cherubim and Seraphim, sing in endless praise:
Holy, holy, holy Lord, God of power and might,
heaven and earth are full of your glory.
The glorious company of apostles praise you.
The noble fellowship of prophets praise you.
The white-robed army of martyrs praise you.
Throughout the world the holy Church acclaims you;
Father, of majesty unbounded,
your true and only Son, worthy of all worship,
and the Holy Spirit, advocate and guide.
You, Christ, are the king of glory,
the eternal Son of the Father.
When you became man to set us free
you did not shun the Virgin's womb.

You overcame the sting of death
and opened the kingdom of heaven to all believers.
You are seated at God's right hand in glory.
We believe that you will come and be our judge.
Come then, Lord, and help your people,
bought with the price of your own blood,
and bring us with your saints
to glory everlasting.
Te Deum, from the *Book of Common Prayer*

Summary and Path for Renewal

Reading about August Herman Franke and German Pietism is somewhat akin to discovering an unknown link in the family to an historical celebrity through Ancestry.com. For Americans, it would be like finding you were related to George Washington or Benjamin Franklin. Franke's story is inspiring and instructive. His entrepreneurial and visionary gifts built a ministry that had impact throughout Europe and America. His school for training ministers required both rigorous study and compassionate service to the young and the poor. What a great discovery in our family tree!

Modern Evangelicals have a rich heritage in Pietism. The core values and practices of 16th and 17th Century German Pietists ring true with us. Promoting small home groups, serving the poor in Jesus' name, and holy living are characteristics that Franke promoted and we still practice. Above all, we share the core conviction that a personal relationship with Christ and a heartfelt faith expressed in the way we live is authentic biblical Christianity.

But along with the rich correctives of our tradition, we have also inherited the Pietist challenges of sentimentality and individualism, especially in our modern American culture. In this chapter, I have attempted to trace our story, celebrate the strength of our tradition, and point out our liabilities. Renewal in this arena is challenging. I have found individualistic values to be fiercely protected. Any critique I have offered which challenges a personal perspective and approach to faith has always been met with ready opposition. But the state of our churches and our worship demands that Christian leaders wrestle with these issues and have the courage to ask the questions. American Evangelicals need to mature and move beyond our individualistic conceptions of faith and worship. In particular, I recommend that we:

- Search for songs and hymns that employ corporate language rather than exclusively personal words. Find a healthy balance between corporate and personal expressions. Use fewer personal songs and we will find that their meaning and impact is raised. Less will be more.

- Use language carefully in worship elements other than just the songs within the service. Look for corporate expressions in prayers, calls to worship, and especially in the sermon focus.

- Reflect on the idea of doing worship as "God's Story" and begin to incorporate those ideas in planning, including songs, readings, and sermons.

- Visit liturgical churches and worship with an open mind. Observe the richness of the words they sing, read, and pray. Consider how some of the content of their services might enrich ours.

- Incorporate ancient forms, including creeds and prayers, from time to time in the service. We may find that the richness of the ancient texts expressed with the heartfelt fervor of the people will be a powerful experience. The ancient forms may prove to be a helpful antidote to our individualistic tendencies in worship.

Finally, in some respects, the historic Lutheran Pietists had it all. They believed in an authentic, "born-again" faith, Bible reading and study in small groups, the pursuit of a holy life, service to their neighbors, and evangelistic fervor. Along with those values which today's Evangelicals cherish deeply, they had a worship experience which kept them deeply rooted in the historic faith and served as a corrective against individualistic liabilities.

They may serve as helpful role models for modern Evangelicals as well.

Questions for Reflection:
1. What values does your church share with historic Lutheran Pietism? Do the similarities surprise you?

2. Do you agree that contemporary American culture is a "culture of Narcissism?"

3. Do you agree with Robert Webber that corporate worship is "doing God's story?"

4. Are you personally resistant to using formal liturgical elements such as creeds, the *Te Deum,* or other set prayers in worship? Why or why not?

5. Are you or others in your church resistant to liturgical innovation because it might appear "too Catholic" or "too Lutheran?" Do you consider that reasoning to be a valid argument against using historic liturgy?

6. What is the ratio of personal to corporate songs that your congregation typically uses in worship?

Suggested Reading:
Bellah, Robert N., et. al., *Habits of the Heart: Individualism and Commitment in American Life,* (New York: Harper and Row, 1985).

Brown, Dale W., *Understanding Pietism*, Nappanee, IN: Evangel Publishing, 1996.

Lasch, Christopher, *The Culture of Narcissism: American Life in an Age of Diminishing Expectations,* (New York: W.W. Norton & Company, 1979).

Sattler, Gary R., *God's Glory, Neighbor's Good,* (Chicago: Covenant Press, 1982).

Stoeffler, F. Earnest, *The Rise of Evangelical Pietism,* (Leiden, Netherlands: E.J. Brill, 1965).

_____ *German Pietism During the Eighteenth Century,* (Leiden, Netherlands: E.J. Brill, 1973).

Strom, Jonathan, Lehmann, Hartmut, and Van Horn Melton, James, eds., *Pietism in Germany and North America 1680-1820,* (Burlington, VT: Ashgate Publishing Company, 2009).

Ward, W.R., *The Protestant Evangelical Awakening,* (Cambridge: Cambridge University Press, 1992).

_____ *Early Evangelicalism: A Global Intellectual History,* 1670-1789, (Cambridge: Cambridge University Press, 2006).

Revivalism's Legacy

"Lord, whence are those blood-drops all the way
That mark out the mountain's track?"
"They were shed for one who had gone astray
Ere the Shepherd could bring him back."
"Lord, whence are Thy hands so rent and torn?"
"They're pierced tonight by many a thorn."

"The Ninety and Nine"
Words by Elizabeth C. Clephane, 1868
Music spontaneously improvised by Ira. D. Sankey, 1874

I was only five years old when my brother told me I was going to hell. Older brothers are like that. He had just prayed to receive Christ as his personal Savior in Sunday School and was pleased to inform me of my fate since I had not yet "prayed the sinner's prayer." This, of course, was very upsetting to me and I went crying to my mom. She explained salvation to me as best she could for a five-year-old to understand and led me in the prayer. This put my brother at bay for a while and ruined his fun. My mom was pleased because she believed that her youngest was now a Christian.

But it didn't really stick. I had done what I was told to do, but I never really felt or heard the Lord's compelling call to me through the whole incident. A year later, when I was six years old, the message struck home. Our little Bible Baptist Church in Alamagordo, New Mexico was holding revival meetings. As usual, when the doors of the church were open, our family was there. I don't remember much from the meeting. I'm sure we sang a bunch of gospel songs from *The Tabernacle Hymnal*, took an offering, and set the preacher loose. It was the same message my mom had told me a year earlier. But this preacher put it across with urgency and fervency. He was hell-fire-and-brimstone (as many of them were back in those days) and his depiction of an eternity of punishment in flames had dramatic effect on me. This I do know: it was that night that I felt and knew God loved *me* and that Jesus died for *my* sins. I went forward at the invitation hymn and prayed once more to receive Christ. This time, I felt it in my heart.

Revivalism's Model: Moody and Sankey in England

The roots of the modern revival movement date back to the first half of the nineteenth century. But the ideal model for organization and methodology came from a former Chicago businessman and a gifted singer in the last quarter of that century. Surprisingly, their most successful enterprise nearly failed before it began. In June of 1873, evangelist Dwight L. Moody (1837-1899) and his song leader Ira D. Sankey (1840-1908) departed for England in order to conduct an evangelism campaign. They had been invited by Cuthbert Bainbridge, a wealthy layman and William Pennefather, a well-known evangelical Anglican minister. Along with the invitation, they had been guaranteed enough of a stipend to bring their families with them. Upon arrival, however, they were informed that both of their benefactors had died during their transatlantic passage. Their circumstances were anything but encouraging. They had no one to greet them, no invitations to pursue, and very little money on hand with which to support themselves. When Moody left New York, he had been in a hurry and distracted by the adventure which lay before him. He had failed to read the mail he had collected there and just stuffed it in with the rest of his luggage. They disembarked at Liverpool and got a room at the Northwestern Hotel. That night, the evangelist and his musical partner discovered a small ray of hope. Sankey related the details later in his memoirs:

> As Mr. Moody was looking over some letters which he had received in New York before sailing, and which had remained unread, he found one from the secretary of the Young Men's

Christian Association at York, asking him if he ever came to England again, to come there and speak for the Association. "Here is a door," said Moody to me after reading the letter, "which is partly open, and we will go there and begin our work."[1]

Invited, but unexpected, the ministry got off to a slow start in York. It wasn't a good time to start a campaign, they were told. Most of the people were away at seaside. According to Sankey, the first meeting was attended by less than fifty people who all sat in the back. Moody pressed on by announcing daily noon-time prayer meetings and Bible studies. It was at one of those meetings that Moody and Sankey secured the friendship and support of F. B. Meyer who would later become one of the most influential Evangelicals in England. Meyer's support was instrumental and the York meetings began to blossom with success and impact. By the time they left for Sunderland three weeks later, the team was beginning to attract enough attention to establish an itinerary. In Sunderland, they invited Henry Moorhouse, a popular and influential minister, to join them in their campaign efforts. Moody had met Moorhouse in Chicago and his endorsement and participation helped shore up the meetings in Sunderland when enthusiasm began to wane.

Moody and Sankey were never quite alone in their endeavors. Their friendship with publisher R. C. Morgan of London was instrumental in promoting their reputation and campaign through his periodical, *The Christian,* the entire time that they were in Great Britain. It was in Sunderland that Morgan suggested Sankey publish some of his most popular gospel songs in a little pamphlet for the people to use during the meetings. Morgan did indeed publish the songs under the title *Sacred Songs and Solos.* The little pamphlets eventually expanded into a songbook that progressed through multiple editions. The songbook would quickly become so popular that the royalties Sankey received from the endeavor

---

[1] Ira. D. Sankey, *My Life and the Story of the Gospel Hymns,* (New York: Harper and Brothers Publishers, 1906) 38.

would support him throughout his life and make him a wealthy man.

After Sunderland, the team moved on to Newcastle. They were beginning to find a rhythm to their work as their reputation and effectiveness grew. It was at Newcastle that Sankey organized his first choir for the campaign. It was there, too, that the singer found nearly equal billing with his partner as promotions declared that "Moody would preach the gospel and Sankey would sing the gospel."[2] The two were a true complementary team. Their gifts and sensitivity converged perhaps most effectively at the climax of the meetings where Moody would give an invitation to respond to the gospel by having people stand and come forward to an "inquiry room" while Sankey led an appropriate and sympathetic hymn. They would hold twice daily meetings where the gospel was preached and sung and an invitation given. They would also meet with affinity groups, holding sessions for men, women, children, and laborers. Biographer, James F. Findlay, Jr. described the team at this point:

> ...success emerged out of a gradual and rather complex process. Moody's imagination and ability to improvise effectively when faced with novel situations, his friendships with people in the evangelical community who were in a position to help him, and his optimistic spirit which carried him through the initial period of frustration all played a part. Given time to learn though trial and error, he was able to move from the edge of disaster to eventual success and fame. By the time the mission in Newcastle was completed he had become, legitimately, a professional revivalist.[3]

Moody and Sankey's greatest success would come, however, in Scotland where they would spend five months. Their first stop was the large port city of Edinburgh. They preached in churches and secular halls, eventually securing the use of the 6,000 seat

---

[2] William G. McLoughlin, Jr. *Modern Revivalism: Charles Grandison Finney to Billy Graham,* (Eugene, OR: Wipf & Stock Publishers, 1959, 2004) 234.

[3] Findlay, James F. *Dwight L. Moody: American Evangelist* (Eugene, OR: Wipf & Stock Publishers, 1969, 2007) 153.

Corn Exchange. Their meetings were frequently crowded and overflowing.

Sankey was especially anxious about his ministry of music in Scotland, which was predominately Presbyterian and at that time restricted their singing exclusively to acapella psalms. Sankey didn't sing psalms; his stock and trade were gospel hymns and songs which he accompanied himself on a portable organ. In an Edinburgh meeting, he encountered Dr. Horatius Bonar, a highly esteemed minister, poet, and writer of hymn texts.[4] In Sankey's words, he sang "with fear and trembling" the night the minister attended. Much to his relief, Bonar was quite pleased and affirmed the gospel singer's efforts.[5] While Moody and Sankey did encounter some ministerial resistance in Scotland, it was overcome by the enthusiasm of the people. Prior to their arrival in 1873, the churches in Scotland had experienced deep divisions over theology and methodology. They needed a catalyst to bring them together and Moody and Sankey's unorthodox, simple, and sincere message hit the mark.

From Edinburgh, they moved on to Glasgow, another large industrial city. There, they experienced similar success. They rented and filled the Crystal Palace, equal to Edinburgh's Corn Exchange in its capacity. Moody and Sankey's schedule was grueling with meetings conducted throughout the week, with only Mondays off for rest. Moody even reached out to the academic community and held sessions with learned faculty – quite a feat for a man with only an eighth-grade education. Their efforts were not without criticism, but by the time they left Scotland in April of 1874, they were true celebrities. From that point on, Moody and Sankey had the advantage of being well-known whenever they would launch a new campaign.

The men had intended to stay in Great Britain for only three months. But their success in Scotland encouraged them to push on in itinerant ministry, reaching smaller cities and Ireland before returning to England in December of 1874. There, they campaigned in the industrial centers of Manchester, Sheffield,

---

[4] Bonar wrote over 600 hymns, his most well-known being, *Here, O My Lord, I See Thee Face to Face.*

[5] Sankey, 60-62.

Birmingham, and Liverpool before coming to London in July, 1875. Their four-month mission in London cultivated the same level of enthusiasm as their efforts in Scotland. Even Charles Spurgeon, the enormously popular Baptist pastor of the Metropolitan Tabernacle, gave them positive support from his pulpit and in his magazine, *The Sword and Trowel.*[6] By the time Moody and Sankey arrived back in England, the machinery of their operation had become truly immense. Through Moody's charisma and business know-how, he was able to recruit a large number of local ministers to assist him in the spiritual matters of the revival campaigns. Devout businessmen led the efforts to arrange logistics to raise the massive amount of capital necessary for each endeavor. Moody had a tabernacle built in Liverpool to accommodate 7,000 people at a cost of $17,000. In London, the final cost for the city campaign rose to an astounding $160,000. On the first night of meetings in that city, over 12,000 people crowded into Agricultural Hall.[7]

It is exceedingly difficult to assess the success or failure of Moody and Sankey's campaign in Great Britain. It is probably true that most of his audience were churched people. In fact, Moody would complain from time to time about the lack of non-Christians in his meetings. Local church statistics during those years also do not seem to indicate that there was a large surge in membership rolls as one might expect as a consequence of the revival meetings. In a broad sense, the campaign raised the level of religious enthusiasm in churches, both in England and in Scotland. With the popularity of *Sacred Songs and Solos* and Sankey's role of "singing the gospel," his place as an equal partner with Moody was also established. Through the enormous success of their sojourn in Great Britain, Moody and Sankey returned home to the United States as popular religious heroes, where they effectively leveraged their standing in mass evangelism until 1880. William G. McLoughlin, Jr.'s exhaustive study, *Modern Revivalism,*

---

[6]<http://www.spurgeon.org/sermons/1239.htm> Accessed January 24, 2014. <http://www.spurgeon.org/s_and_t/moody75.htm> Accessed July 11, 2013.

[7] Findlay, 170-171.

offered this important assessment of Moody and Sankey's remarkable campaign in Great Britain:

> The trip to Britain…had a profound influence upon the subsequent course of modern revivalism. The system which Moody worked out in Britain and the factors which made him successful there were in large measure the same as those which were to shape the course of revivalism in the United States during the next half century.[8]

Early American Affinity with Revivalism

Revivalism has always found a ready home in America. Our national individualistic DNA resonated with revivalism's appeal for personal salvation. But the approach and core values of modern revivalism which began in the early nineteenth century differed significantly from America's original revival, The First Great Awakening (c. 1734-1758). The first movement was firmly rooted in Pietism with the emphasis on the necessity of a personal conversion experience. The two most significant preachers associated with the awakening were pastor Jonathan Edwards (1703-1758) and evangelist George Whitefield (1714-1770). Both Edwards and Whitefield were Calvinists who emphasized the sovereign work of God in bringing sinners to salvation. They preached both the judgment and mercy of God. There were no altar calls or prescribed sinner's prayers. But the results of the juxtaposition of God's righteous judgment and loving mercy in their preaching had a dramatic effect on the hearers. Weeping, moaning, and other physical manifestations were not uncommon from those who were under conviction. Ministers allowed the Spirit to do his work, encouraging those under conviction to seek God and his mercy in prayer until they found peace. Those who eventually came to a place of peace through experiencing the forgiveness of God were considered converted and added to the church rolls.

---

[8] McLoughlin, Jr, 178.

In 1801, in the frontier of wild Kentucky, an estimated 20,000 people converged on Cane Ridge to hear evangelistic preaching. Presbyterian pastor James McGready (1763-1817), empowered by an intense prayer life, had established an effective ministry a year before with three churches in the region which was known for its violence and debauchery. He was invited to Cane Ridge to conduct meetings in April of 1801. The attendance at the open-air meetings was so large and unexpected that additional preachers were required to engage the crowds. The message was essentially the same as what Edwards and Whitefield had delivered a generation before along the Eastern Seaboard. As in the First Great Awakening, there were no prescribed sinner's prayers and no invitation as we would know them today. But an area near the preacher was designated as the place where those under conviction could come to "pray through" until they found peace. As in the First Great Awakening, church rolls grew significantly and social vices dramatically declined.

But with the advent of the ministry of Charles Finney (1792-1875) in upstate New York, new paradigms of revivalism began to be established. Finney was both lionized and demonized in his day and in history. He is perhaps the most polarizing figure in American evangelical history. Finney began his career as an attorney. He possessed a sharp mind and a penetrating gaze that served him well in his short-lived law career. But in 1821, he had a profound conversion experience that would reshape the purpose and direction of his life. He prepared himself to be a Presbyterian minister and was ordained in 1824. Calvinism, which emphasizes the sovereign election of God for salvation, was pervasive at the time. But Finney rejected what he perceived as the limitations of God's exclusive initiative in the salvation process and actively cultivated a public response of the individual to the gospel.

Charles G. Finney

Events early in his preaching ministry would establish his aggressive approach in evangelism that would eventually become known as "new measures." Since Finney had no formal training in ministry, he determined to begin in small towns rather than large cities. In 1824, he began preaching in Evans Mills, NY after securing an invitation by the Baptist and Congregational congregations there. Shortly after he began, Finney became irritated by the affirmations that he received from the people. His desire was not to please people but to bring them under conviction of their need for Christ. Like a seasoned attorney trying to secure a decision from a jury, he proceeded to press them logically to make a choice for or against Christ. At the climax of his message, he demanded that all who would follow Christ should stand. The people had never experienced such a challenge and must have been shocked. Not one of them stirred. Finney's reaction was unsparing: "Then you are committed. You have taken your stand. You have rejected Christ and his gospel; and ye are witnesses one against the other, and God is witness against you all." He continued to press them and they all got up to walk out, seething in anger. When they were almost out the door, Finney called after them, "I am sorry for you; and will preach to you once more, the Lord willing, tomorrow night."[9]

It's a wonder that they didn't tar and feather him and run him out of town on a rail on the spot. It wasn't that some folks hadn't considered violent options. One man planned to come to the meeting with a gun to kill the evangelist. But the anger of the townspeople soon changed as a heavy spirit of conviction came

---

[9] Garth M. Rosell & Richard A. G. Dupuis, editors, *The Memoirs of Charles Finney: The Complete Restored Text*, (Grand Rapids, MI: Zondervan, 1989) 65-67.

upon them. In the days that followed, many would weep and wail under conviction at the meetings where Finney preached. And many made public decisions to follow Christ.

In stark opposition to Calvinist understanding and practice, Finney used his persuasive powers as a former attorney to convince people of their need of salvation. He shifted the emphasis in the salvation equation from God's sovereign initiative to human individual response. Because his approach was humanistic, he employed logic and emotional persuasion. Cynics would say that he was manipulative.

He worked with Thomas Hastings (1784-1872), composer of the tune for "Rock of Ages," as his musical partner to serve in his evangelistic services. Finney also institutionalized the invitation hymn, where those responding to the gospel call were invited to a "mourner's bench" or "anxious bench." Those who came forward were led to make a decision for Christ either at the church or later in their homes as the evangelist would visit them.

Finney was unapologetic in using all means at his disposal in order to bring people to Christ. Like a politician, he would campaign against the evils of the Devil and persuade people to "vote in the Lord Jesus Christ as the governor of the Universe."[10] He intentionally employed threats and entertainment as he sought to engage his audience through stories and theatrics. McLaughlin summarized Finney's approach and values:

> Finney believed that "The great end for which Christian ministry was appointed is to glorify God in the salvation of souls" and therefore that "all ministers should be revival ministers and all preaching should be revival preaching." Preaching was good if it won souls and bad if it did not. To be practical, said Finney, revival preaching had to attract attention. To do this it had to be exciting.[11]

As revival fires eventually cooled in upstate New York, Charles Finney considered pastoral ministry in New York City but was

---

[10] McLaughlin, 87.
[11] *Ibid.*, 87.

unable to fulfill his intention because of illness. He eventually redirected his career to education and established a school for evangelists at Oberlin College in 1835.

The Emergence of the Prominent Songleader

What Finney started with the emergence of new paradigms in revivalism, Moody and Sankey perfected in modern revivalism with their venture in Great Britain. Moody was, at heart, a practical businessman and he would use every appropriate means to meet the end of saving souls. He and Sankey would create an atmosphere that was conducive to the reception of the gospel in the hearts of his hearers. The services began with a full hour of congregational singing, choir specials, personal testimonies, and heart-rending solos. The effect was dramatic:

> The greatest power of the music...has lain in the sweeping, surging, irresistible, overwhelming, singing of the congregations...And you, too, though you have only gone in as an indifferent and critical spectator, before you know it you too are drawn into the enchanted current, and are being borne with strange intoxication on the bosom of the wild but wondrous song...Only he knows that who has himself stood in the midst of the great multitude, awed and borne away by the strange power of its mighty choruses.[12]

Unlike Finney, Moody was plain-spoken and avoided sensational theatrics in his speaking. But he turned his song leader loose to move people through his gospel songs and hymns. Moody and Sankey's methodology resonated with the romantic sentimentalism of the Victorian Age. Sankey's solos were often tear-jerking ballads. Among the songs that he sang was "Room Among the Angels," a song about an abused little girl who dies and goes to heaven. Similar in sentiment was "Little Willie" by P. P. Bliss:

---

[12] Findlay, 288-289.

"But she told me, I remember, once while sitting on her knee;
That the angels never weary watching over her and me;
And if we're good (and mamma told me just the same before),
They will let us into heaven when they see us at the door."[13]

More typical, however, was one of Moody's favorite invitational
hymns, as described by Sankey:

> One of the most impressive occasions on which this hymn
> was sung was in the Agricultural Hall in London, in 1874,
> when Mr. Gladstone [the Prime Minister] was present. At the
> close of his sermon Mr. Moody asked the congregation to
> bow their heads, while I sang "Almost Persuaded." The
> stillness of death prevailed throughout the audience of over
> fifteen thousand, as souls were making their decisions for
> Christ."

Almost persuaded now to believe;
Almost persuaded Christ to receive;
Seems now some soul to say,
Go, Spirit, go Thy way,
Some more convenient day
On Thee I'll call...

Almost persuaded, harvest is past!
Almost persuaded, doom comes at last!
Almost cannot avail;
Almost is but to fail!
Sad, sad, that bitter wail
Almost, but lost! [14]

P. P. Bliss

Moody and Sankey's campaigns had lasting impact on the
evangelical churches of their day. Though the number of
conversions recorded with the campaign weren't always reflected

---

[13] McLaughlin, 236.
[14] Sankey, 112.

in the growth of local church rolls, it was true that the methods which so powerfully moved the church-goers who attended the revivals also changed their expectations for weekly worship. Ministers who had come under revivalistic influence crafted their services, including the simple format, testimonies, and the use of gospel hymns and songs, to try and reproduce the excitement that people had experienced in Moody and Sankey's meetings.

Twentieth Century Revivalism

After Moody and Sankey, many revival teams effectively ministered during the sentimental Victorian era. Evangelists who followed their lead included Sam Jones (1847-1906), Rueben Archer Torrey (1856-1928), and J. Wilbur Chapman (1859-1915). Like Moody, each partnered with an effective song leader. Most also promoted temperance themes, denouncing liquor, smoking, the theatre, card-playing, and dancing. The effect was lasting on Evangelicals well into the twentieth century. When I attended Biola College in the 1970's (which was co-founded by Torrey), I was required to sign an agreement stating that I would abstain from all of those activities. A church that I served as lead pastor from 2012-2016 had a church covenant containing temperance prohibitions rooted in their revivalist tradition.

The ministry of Billy Sunday (1863-1935) deserves special recognition. The former professional baseball player was, by far, the most successful evangelist in the first decades of the twentieth century. According to Elmer Towns and Vernon Whaley, "He preached in more than 300 evangelistic campaigns in every major city in the country, and more than 593,000 made decisions for Christ as a result of his preaching."[15] In many of the cities he ministered, special "Billy Sunday Tabernacles" had to be built to accommodate the large crowds that he attracted.

---

[15] Elmer L. Towns and Vernon M. Whaley, *Worship Through the Ages,* (Nashville: B & H Publishing Group, 2012) 239-240.

Like Moody, Billy Sunday built an efficient revival machine to handle logistics and his musical partner was Homer Rodeheaver (1880-1955), as much the equal to Sankey in musical ability and entrepreneurial enterprise. His speaking style, however, was without doubt the most theatrical of all revivalists up to his time: shouting, running, jumping – in effect, using his prowess as an athlete to get his message across. Billy Sunday

Billy Sunday's Physical Style

revival meetings would rival the entertainment of any circus or vaudeville act. Rodeheaver's talents were a good match for his partner. He was master-of-ceremonies, trombone soloist, and choir director all wrapped up into one. The music was greatly entertaining and almost the equal draw of Sunday's electrifying sermons. Billy Sunday sought to merge American patriotism and the gospel. His popular ministry was significant in propelling the Temperance Movement to success in its instituting of Prohibition. Scandal often shadowed him, however, because of the large sums of money involved in the enterprise, and because of his extravagant lifestyle and his children's prodigal ways. But none of his domestic troubles seemed to have a negative impact on his effectiveness as a popular revivalist. Sunday is generally regarded positively by American Evangelicals and he profoundly impacted what they would expect in a religious service.

Billy Graham's (1918-2018) ministry would use most of the methodologies he inherited from Moody/Sankey and Sunday/Rodeheaver. But unlike some of his predecessors, Graham cultivated a reputation beyond reproach except among the most separatist fundamentalists. Even the most jaded non-believers held him in high regard. His legacy of integrity is remarkable in that he never diluted the gospel to attract more people. Graham utilized Cliff Barrows (1923-2016) as a master-of-ceremonies, song leader, and choir director. George Beverly Shea (1909-2013) was his favored soloist, though he used other musical celebrities in his crusades. The most significant innovation that Billy Graham used was religious broadcasting. I recall watching his crusades on television in my home many times. I always became emotional during the singing of "Just As I Am" as hundreds of people would stream to the platform in response to the invitation. The Billy Graham Association also started a film company in 1953, Worldwide Films. The movies typically depicted stories of people in moral crises who would come to a Billy Graham Crusade and make a decision for Christ. Like Graham's sermons, the films presented the gospel simply in an emotionally compelling story.

It seems there are no American evangelists on the horizon who come close to the stature of a Graham, Sunday, or Moody. Still, modern revivalism is perhaps the most influential movement in shaping the contours of Free Church worship in the nineteenth through the twenty-first centuries. If revivalism were a house, Whitefield and Edwards poured the footings and laid the foundation. Finney framed the structure and Moody/Sankey finished it. Sunday remodeled it and Graham sold it to a new generation. We bought it and have lived in it.

Modern Revivalism's Impact on Evangelical Worship

Revivalism has many children. It has many critics as well. Contemporary manifestations of revivalistic meetings such as the "stadium events" of the 1990's Promise Keeper rallies, Greg Laurie's Harvest Crusades, Women of Faith Events, and Passion Conferences are effective in evangelism of the lost and encouragement of believers. Not only have the methods of revivalists since Finney brought converts into the Kingdom of God, they have also raised many questions and shaped the way we worship on Sunday mornings. Revivalistic events are an effective merging of contemporary culture and historic revivalism models. We need, however, to consider the full impact of revivalism upon the health of the church.

In recent years, much has been written to criticize what is labeled as a "reductionist" or "minimalist" concept of Christian conversion that finds its roots in revivalism. The push-back is a necessary and overdue correction. So many of our so-called conversions that came from a simple reciting of the prescribed "sinner's prayer" have failed to bear lasting fruit. J. D. Greear addressed the issue in 2013 through his popular book entitled *Stop Asking Jesus Into Your Heart.*[16] A more complete critique and corrective can be found in Gordon T. Smith's work in which he presents and unpacks seven essential biblical elements of Christian conversion.[17] The conversation regarding the essence of Christian conversion is closely related to the nature and impact of revivalism and it is perhaps long overdue. Nevertheless, the focus of our consideration in this book is limited to the significant impact of revivalism on evangelical corporate worship.

Evangelism as Priority One

It was Finney who articulated the winning of souls as the first priority of the church. By soul-winning, he meant bringing sinners to a point of decision to accept Christ as their personal Savior. Generations of Evangelicals would resonate with Finney. But soul-winning, as Finney and his revivalist offspring defined and modeled it, falls short of the Great Commission – to make disciples. The failure to make a distinction between decisions made and lives transformed through discipleship has impoverished and stunted the maturity of the American evangelical church.

In order to fulfill the first priority of revivalistic churches, worship services were modeled after mass evangelism events. The structure of the service, architecture of the sanctuary, and role expectations for both preacher and song-leader all took their cues from revival meetings. Perhaps the most obvious form that was inherited from revivalism was the invitation following the sermon.

---

[16] J.D. Greear, *Stop Asking Jesus Into Your Heart,* (Nashville: B & H Publishing Group, 2013).

[17] Gordon T. Smith, *Beginning Well* (Downers Grove: Intervarsity Press, 2001) and *Transforming Conversion: Rethinking the Language and Contours of Christian Conversion,* (Grand Rapids: Baker Academic, 2010).

In many modern evangelical churches, the invitation has fallen out of favor since the late twentieth century. Charismatic churches have effectively translated the closing hymn from a simple invitation for salvation or rededication to "ministry time" where people come forward for any spiritual need. But in non-Charismatic churches, response to public invitations for salvation has simply waned in the last thirty years. As a result, many pastors have ceased giving them.

The failure to make a distinction between decisions made and lives transformed …has impoverished and stunted the American evangelical church.

The mandate of the Great Commission is to make disciples rather than simply get people to say a prayer. The quest for discipleship is holistic while the invitation to "make a decision to accept Christ" is just a beginning. If discipleship is the church's mandate, then that is where the focus of the weekly sermon should generally lie. Preaching for discipleship does not preclude evangelism, but "soul-winning" should not be the sole focus, as Finney would have had it. Christian discipleship implies transformation. A *changed life* should be the focus of the church's teaching and preaching if we are to remain true to the Great Commission's mandate. Transformation will happen when people respond in obedience to what the Spirit is saying to them through the Word of God. Response to the Word in worship is not optional. It is necessary if biblical discipleship is to happen.

From time to time, when the text seems right, I cast my net broader to challenge those present who may not be believers and extend an invitation to receive Christ. But typically, evangelism happens most often in the context of relationships outside of the church walls, in personal counseling, or in small groups rather than in corporate worship. I do not think it is wise to extend a revivalistic invitation to receive Christ every Sunday. If that becomes the regular pattern, believers feel relieved from the obligation to respond to the Word. It's as though the Christian can check out at that time (except for praying for the lost to respond) thinking, "I don't have to respond to this, the preacher isn't talking to me." Such a conception of corporate worship undermines the call to holistic discipleship. And it is far removed from the biblical description of the first church's gatherings we find in Acts 2:42: "They devoted themselves to the apostles' teaching and to fellowship, to the breaking of bread and to prayer." Evangelistic invitations should not be prohibited. We should, however, be carefully reflective about using them at an appropriate time rather than planning one after each sermon as a matter of course.

The Quick Fix

True revivals like the First Great Awakening are sovereign movements of God that happen outside of the planning and programming of humans. You cannot schedule an outpouring of the Holy Spirit. We have, of course, cultivated confusion by calling our mass evangelism meetings "revivals." It is true that God works through mass evangelism, often very powerfully. But a series of meetings is not the same as a sovereign movement of the Spirit of God that convicts sinners and renews the Church. Historically, true revivals often started unexpectedly and waned without warning – usually lasting months or years and spanning denominations and geography.

One of the legacies of revivalism and the scheduling and programming of "revival meetings" is the tendency among Evangelicals to crave the "quick fix" that it offers. I remember praying for years for someone that I loved to return to the Lord. From time to time he would attend a service and when the invitation came, I prayed fervently that he would respond. He never did. The dramatic change that I was praying would occur in one moment happened, rather, over a span of many years. Eventually, he came back to Christ. Revivalism tends to cultivate an appetite and expectation for the dramatic conversion. Sometimes they do occur. But God's work in people often happens over time rather than in just a moment.

Recognition of corporate worship's role in the long journey of spiritual formation will shape the values and ultimately the substance of what happens in a service.

Though corporate worship needs no other justification than its own intrinsic worth, it remains a powerful factor in the spiritual formation of the congregation and its members. Recognition of corporate worship's role in the *long journey* of spiritual formation will shape the values and ultimately the substance of what happens in a service. Reminding pastors, worship planners, and leaders that spiritual formation cultivated in corporate worship happens over time will relieve and correct the notion that every week has to be dynamic and produce a dramatic effect on the people. Philosopher James K. A. Smith is insightful:

> Worship is the area in which God recalibrates our hearts, reforms our desires, and rehabituates our loves. Worship isn't just something we do; it is where God does something to us.

Worship is the heart of discipleship because it is the gymnasium in which God retrains our hearts.[18]

For many in our evangelical churches, such a perspective would be a significant and welcome paradigm shift.

Structure

For the last forty years, the evangelical church has fought over musical styles in worship. Sadly, for many, it has become the main issue in corporate worship. Our preoccupation with musical style has distracted us from considering other areas that also have impoverished our worship. The structure of our worship service is a reflection of what we believe should happen when we gather to engage with God. Most non-liturgical evangelical churches typically follow the model of a revivalistic service:

Prelude
Greetings and Call to Worship
Hymn/Song Set
Welcome and Announcements
Special Music
Offering
Hymn or Song
Message
Invitation or Hymn/Song of Response
Benediction

Churches that utilize a revivalist format usually have little time for Scripture reading and prayer in their corporate worship. There are, of course, exceptions. But the model does not promote an emphasis on these two elements which historically have been essential for the church since its beginnings in Acts. And sadly, the Lord's Table, when it is observed, is sometimes viewed as

---

[18] James K. A. Smith, *You Are What You Love: The Spiritual Power of Habit* (Grand Rapids: Brazos Press, 2016) 77.

more of a bother than essential to the spiritual health of the congregation.

There are other structural models for corporate worship design besides revivalistic that would enhance meaning in evangelical services. Charismatic churches have a structure for their musical medleys that progressively move from celebration to intimacy. But aside from intentional design in the music set, their services still follow the basic revivalist trajectory of music – message – response. Liturgical churches generally use what Robert Webber termed the historic "four-fold" structure. There is a logical and relational dynamic to the flow of the service. It begins with *Gathering,* in which the people are called to worship and their focus is directed God-ward. From the gathering, worship moves to the *Service of the Word*, where Scripture is read and preached. The apex of the service is *the Lord's Table.* In non-liturgical churches where the Lord's Table is not observed weekly, Webber suggests some sort of *Response to the Word* that would include a relational component with other worshippers. Finally, the service is closed with *Sending* the congregation out to love and serve the Lord in the world.[19]

Non-liturgical worship planners can also enrich their services if they will give attention to issues of dialogue and flow. Worship should be a relational conversation between God's *revelation* of himself and his Word, and the *response* of his people. When services are planned with *revelation* and *response* in mind, each element takes on real meaning. In addition, because corporate worship is viewed as a relational dialogue, each element should be planned to segue into the next as a conversation would.

> *Worship should be a relational conversation between God's revelation of himself and his Word with the response of the people.*

---

[19] Constance Cherry's book, *The Worship Architect* is very effective in developing the four-fold model along with plenty of ideas for implementation. (Grand Rapids, MI: Baker Academic, 2010)

Such a service, even with simple revivalist structure, can be infused with life and meaning. (See Appendix A, *Creating Flow in a Worship Set*, for more technical ideas on worship development.)

Worship as Entertainment

Moody's ways of engaging the people made a strong impact in Scotland when he arrived there in 1874. One Scottish clergyman reflected that the revivalist's methods "have led many of us to feel the need of changing somewhat our modes of operation and of seeking to improve our stereotyped Sabbath services...The people will demand this at our hands all over the country."[20] Since then, for nearly 150 years, Free Church Evangelicals have followed suit, adapting contemporary entertainment forms into corporate worship.

Fifty years before Moody, Finney intentionally directed all attention to the platform. Even though the revivalist never settled in New York, he designed the worship space of the Broadway Tabernacle, which he intended to pastor, so that all could see him on the platform and so that he, in turn, could look directly in their eyes. With the rise of revivalism's popularity in the late nineteenth century, churches began to build their sanctuaries to look like theaters, with sloping floors and proscenium arches framing the platform. Moody's Church in Chicago is a prime example, and many of the churches that were built in that era featured a design borrowed from the theater.[21]

But the greatest impact of revivalism in worship was on the platform. In Moody's day, the innovations were primarily in his plain manner of speaking and especially in Sankey's use of gospel hymns and heart-stirring solos. The audience expected to be moved. Everyone who had a place on the platform had to be able to engage the congregation. After the model of Ira Sankey and Homer Rodeheaver, song-leaders had to smile and to be energetic and entertaining. In my role as a worship leader I have usually led

---

[20] McGloughlin, 206-207.

[21] Jeanne Halgren Kilde, *When Church Became Theatre: The Transformation of Evangelical Architecture and Worship in Nineteenth-Century America* (New York: Oxford University Press, 2002).

congregational singing from the piano. In one church that I served, some people objected because they wanted a "smiling song-leader" conducting the singing standing at the podium rather than what seemed to them as a singing musician doing his "gig" in a barroom! I always found the comparison amusing, not just because I was following Sankey's lead, but also because the church frowned on the use of alcohol. How would they know what a barroom looked like?

The topic of entertainment in worship has been eagerly discussed since evangelical worship renewal efforts began in the late twentieth century. It is an important conversation since much of our popular culture is focused on the entertainment business. The popularity of contemporary Christian music has made the issue all the more critical. Most renewalists have adopted Soren Kierkegaard's concept of worship as theater where God is the audience, worship leaders are prompters, and members of the congregation are the performers.[22] Kierkegaard's concept is very helpful but it needs constant reinforcement because our culture's default is for platform people to become performers and the congregation to become the passive audience. Revivalism did promote active participation during congregational singing, but all other elements of the meeting were expected to be very entertaining. Worship renewal seeks to challenge that paradigm.

---

[22] Quoted in "Who's the Host?" by Emily Brink in *Reformed Worship, Issue #33, September 1994.* https://www.reformedworship.org/article/september-1994/whos-host-we-may-be-getting-carried-away-kierkegaards-analogy. Original source cited: Søren Kierkegaard, *Purity of Heart*, pp. 180-81 (SV XI114-15); reprinted in *Parables of Kierkegaard*, Thomas C. Oden, ed..Accessed 7.18.2017.

There are several practices that musicians, preachers, and other platform leaders can do to combat the entertainment mentality. Certainly, musicians should never bow or acknowledge congregational applause. The congregation also needs to discuss and determine whether applause is appropriate in the worship service. Charismatics sometimes

The topic of entertainment in worship...is an important conversation since much of our popular culture is focused on the entertainment business.

do a "clap offering" after an uplifting, typically upbeat song. This practice is spontaneous and seems to be another cultural way of saying "amen." Clapping of hands, or applause, becomes more problematic when it occurs after a solo or special musical offering. Some churches feel that it is another "amen" expression and affirms the person offering the gift in an expression of loving gratitude and fellowship. Other churches forbid the practice as irreverent and promoting an entertainment mindset. Each congregation will have to reflect carefully on their context and decide on the issue of applause.

Vocalists should also avoid "showing off" their abilities in order to draw attention to themselves. Every singer knows the joy of singing and those who have developed an agile voice may be tempted to test their limits through optional high notes and improvised phrases between the melody lines. The temptation is even stronger if the singer is trying to emulate an artist they heard on a recording. Variations from the melody are only appropriate in leading worship if they assist the congregation in singing better. It is one thing to give your best effort; quite another to seek public admiration for your abilities. Mature vocalists will know when they've crossed the line and leaders need to be ready to correct those who seek glory for themselves. The integrity of corporate worship is at stake!

Stage lighting has become a significant issue since more and more churches are installing sophisticated systems to replicate a concert venue. Technicians need strong guidance here because they will instinctively isolate musicians while leaving the congregation in the dark. The net result is that the congregation will naturally resort to a passive audience role and be readily content to listen rather than participate. After all, that's what the lighting is directing them to do!

Finally, in such patterns, just as musicians need to be credible performers to lead a group of people, so are preachers expected to be performers from this perspective. Musicians perform to facilitate focus on God in their songs; preachers perform in order to draw attention to God's Word. Many object to the idea of musicians or preachers performing in worship, but the vocalist who constantly sings out of tune and the preacher whose message cannot be followed draw attention *away* from God and his Word.[23] Some performance ability is inherent in both roles. Preachers, therefore, should avoid drawing attention to their abilities, but point to Christ. A sense of humor is appropriate, but cultivating "cuteness" is not. Preachers instinctively know whether they are doing it for their own benefit or pointing to God. A mature preacher knows that he or she is accountable to God and approaches the pulpit humbly.

Celebrity Expectations of the Preaching Pastor

One of the most profound and damaging effects of modern revivalism was the rise of the celebrity preacher. People came to expect an exciting sermon and if they didn't get one, they could move on to a church which might have a more entertaining preacher. The negative effects of this expectation for a preacher and church are at least three-fold. First, if the highest expectation for the preaching pastor is his ability to entertain the congregation, it opened the door for preachers who may be otherwise unqualified for the pastoral office. I'm not speaking of formal

---

[23] See Barry Liesch, *The New Worship: Straight Talk on Music and the Church* (Grand Rapids: Baker Books, 2001) p. 121-140 for an excellent discussion on the topic of performance in worship.

credentials or degrees. Too many churches have been stunted in their growth through an immature ministry focused on entertainment from the pulpit. Generally, such a ministry has a unhappy ending as the immature gifted pastor usually self-destructs and may take much of the church along with him. The Scriptures do not prescribe entertainers for pulpit ministry. Sadly, revivalism has introduced entertainment as an expectation in corporate worship and its legacy is a weakened church.

Secondly, if congregations over-value an entertaining speaker, they may also undervalue a mature pastor who may be less engaging in the pulpit. Such a situation lays great undue stress on the pastor and blinds the congregation to the spiritual wealth that he or she may offer. Preachers can and should always work hard on increasing their effectiveness in the pulpit. But not every preacher is good-looking and possesses the "gift of gab." Congregations should be wise and seek a preaching pastor who is spiritually mature and able to preach Scripture so that people will engage and discern the Word of God. Physical appearance and the ability to entertain, while wonderful advantages to have, are not biblical pre-requisites for a preaching ministry.

Finally, I have observed that the tendency to elevate the preacher to the status of celebrity has laid unrealistic expectations on the person. He or she is expected to be the perfect leader of the church. Since the preacher is the shining star in the pulpit, the assumption is that he or she must also be effective in leading the staff, handling administrative details, and counseling the hurting. The pastor, in other words, must be a superman. I have observed that if the preacher is dynamic in the pulpit, his or her weaknesses in other areas are generally ignored to the detriment of the entire ministry. People are reluctant to criticize their celebrity pastor, especially if his giftedness has enabled him to escape scrutiny and to cultivate defensiveness or immaturity.

Churches should realize the dangers that a celebrity complex can bring to a church and take steps to avoid it.

Churches should realize the dangers that a celebrity complex can bring to a church and take steps to avoid it. Pastors who are especially gifted in speaking should take the initiative in making themselves vulnerable to critique in areas where they are weak. Very few can "do it all" with a high level of excellence. If the gifted preacher can't administrate the activity of the organization or lead personnel well, churches should consider allowing another staff person so gifted to handle those roles. Finally, a celebrity complex can be intentionally avoided by sharing some pulpit time with other pastors if it is a multi-staff church.

Sentimentalism

Modern revivalism, with its roots deeply formed in the Victorian soil of the late nineteenth century, breeds sentimentalism. Sentimentalism is more than just a welcome environment for emotional expression. *Sentimentalism equates emotion with substance.* It is feeling for feeling's sake. Certain songs or experiences will spark emotion in the sentimentalist which is equated with authentic worship. The sentimental worshipper comes to expect those kinds of experiences each week. It is an unfortunate dynamic in any congregation. And sentimentalism is not limited to a particular generation. I have observed it in the "Builder Generation" with their insistence on gospel hymns and invitations as well as with "Millennials" who insist on their favorite songs from the Christian radio playlist.

When sentimentalists experience what they want in a worship service, they believe the service was good. When their emotional expectations are not met, they frequently complain and become resistant to anything but what they want. The impediment to renewal is that sentiment is confused with substance. New songs or worship elements, no matter how profound the text or music, are resisted because they do not generate the emotion expected. As a worship leader, I have found sentimentalism to be one of my greatest frustrations because it closes the mind of the worshipper to meaningful innovation.

Overcoming sentimentalism in a congregation requires a great deal of patience. The saying, "You can lead a horse to water, but you can't make it drink," is surely applicable. The worship renewalist who wishes to move his or her congregation away from sentimentalism should develop a thick skin along with a long-term strategy of teaching on the substance and meaning of worship.

Sentimentalism equates emotion with substance.

Develop an intentional preaching or teaching series on worship. Look for "teachable moments" in the weekly service that will inform the congregation of what is being done. Be careful not to bow to sentimentalism but ensure that everything in the service has meaning and substance. Avoid crowd-pleasing emotion for emotion's sake. Certainly, there will be moments in worship that will generate significant emotional response. But it will be because the moment and meaning were right, rather than the result of a play to the crowd. With intention, perseverance, and intention, the worship culture of the congregation will evolve and the people will begin to learn and appreciate true meaning in the service. They will grow beyond the sentimental confusion of emotion with substance and become more mature worshippers.

Preparing Hearts to Hear the Word

Finally, perhaps the most significant impact that modern revivalism has had on evangelical worship is to limit the role of music. For the revivalist, music is powerfully utilitarian. It has no intrinsic value except in what it does in relation to the sermon. I have been told all my life that the role of music in corporate worship was "to prepare the hearts of the people to receive the message." Even Warren Wiersbe, in his commentary on Nehemiah 12, defines the music ministry in his church in the same way: "The musicians had led the congregation in praise and *helped*

bad

prepare them for the hearing of the Word" (emphasis mine). [24] That's what Ira Sankey did for D. L. Moody. Homer Rodeheaver did it for Billy Sunday and Cliff Barrows was the warm-up for Billy Graham. Such a view is terribly unfortunate, though pervasive, and diminishes the rich role that music should have in worship.

Martin Luther's love and appreciation for song in worship is well-known and appreciated even by non-Lutheran Protestants. [25] But before Luther, the Apostle Paul wrote to the Colossians, encouraging them to "Let the word of Christ dwell in you richly, teaching and admonishing one another in all wisdom with psalms, hymns, and spiritual songs, with thankfulness in your hearts to God" (Col. 3:16).

What we sing does matter for the sake of spiritual formation. Song repertoire is one of the most powerful shapers of our spiritual understanding. In the Church's song we express the story and truth of the full gospel and do it in a way that engages our whole being: body, mind, and spirit. My introduction to the doctrine of the Trinity was *Holy, Holy, Holy, Lord God Almighty!* I learned about God's transcendence by singing *"Immortal, Invisible."* *"And Can It Be?"* deepened my understanding of Christian conversion. Everything that we do in corporate worship should form us into maturing disciples of Christ, whether it is singing, prayer, giving of our offerings, hearing the spoken Word, partaking of the Lord's Table, even greeting one another. Singing is only one of several meaningful elements within Christian worship. And I affirm, along with the Apostle Paul and Martin Luther, that it is a wonderful gift and powerful medium in proclaiming God's story in which we have been cast as players.

---

[24] Warren W. Wiersbe, *The Wiersbe Bible Commentary: Old Testament,* (Colorado Springs, CO: David C. Cook, 2007) p. 786.

[25] See especially Lutheran church musician Paul Westermeyer's consideration of Luther's perspective in his book, *Te Deum,* p. 142-149. (Minneapolis, MN: Fortress Press, 1998.) Fred Bock included the following Luther epigram at the beginning of his non-denominational hymnal, *Hymns for the Family of God* (Nashville, TN: Paragon and Associates, 1976): "I am strongly persuaded that after theology there is no art that can be placed on a level with music; for besides theology, music is the only art capable of affording peace and joy of the heart…the devil flees before the sound of music almost as much as before the Word of God."

I know that music has the power to move people. That is one of its fundamental gifts. But music in corporate worship is much more because it carries the gospel itself, with all its transforming power. Like the sermon or even the Lord's Table, the song of the Church has intrinsic worth. When we prescribe and limit the role of worship music to "preparing hearts to receive the message," we strip it of its formational power and simply use it as a manipulation device. And yet for many church people and ministers in the Free Church tradition, that is exactly what is expected of a worship leader or church musician who selects the songs for corporate worship.

There are not many who ask the preaching pastor for a favorite sermon or a message on a favored topic. I know it happens, but probably not as often as favorite song requests are submitted. I'm not suggesting that the songs we sing are more important than the Word that is preached. It is unnecessary and unhelpful to compare. Worship always springs from God's Word. But just as the sermon has worth because it is God's Word and has transformational power, so also the song of the Church has worth because it too, often carries God's Word and its inherent power. The point is simply this: to preach is a pastoral burden and responsibility; to select the music we sing is nothing less. Selecting music and designing corporate worship is a pastoral role and responsibility that worship leaders need to embrace and the Church needs to understand.

It does not mean, however, that only pastors are qualified to select music and design the worship service. Selecting worship music is "pastoral" in that it is a role that has a responsibility for the spiritual nurture of the church. Certainly, pastors should be directly involved in music selection or at least working with the person or persons doing the selection. Whoever selects music takes the responsibility to choose wisely with an eye to worship function and biblical integrity. The spiritual health of the congregation depends upon it.

Summary and Path for Renewal

As the narrative and our historic reflection move closer to our own day, the portraits in our virtual family picture album become more familiar. I heard stories about Moody and Sankey as a child. Many Evangelicals my age and older have sung some of Sankey's songs. My parents heard Billy Sunday and adopted his revivalist mindset and values. Virtually every Evangelical knows who Billy Graham is and has felt his impact in some way. Revivalism fits many of us like a well-worn shoe. But with our familiar comfort we also have the risk of being unable to discern the liabilities of our adopted tradition.

Modern revivalism began with Finney's "new methods" in the early nineteenth century. Moody and Sankey perfected and institutionalized revivalism's methodology which was effectively used for over one hundred years and is still in use today. While it bore fruit in bringing many to Christ (I know a number of people who came to faith through revival meetings) and generating enthusiasm in churches, one of its most significant influences was on the way that Free Church Evangelicals conceived of their worship services. The powerful impact of revival meetings directly influenced the structure and substance of services and the expectations of worshippers on Sunday mornings. Instead of worship services that would shape disciples, people began to expect Sunday services to evangelize the lost.

Revivalism's legacy is pervasive throughout non-liturgical Evangelicalism. Generally, we are unaware of its impact upon us. It is very ingrained and protected by sentiment. Unfortunately, revivalism's influence in worship has impoverished evangelical understanding and practice of corporate worship. Several of the negative outcomes have been explored with suggestions for renewal offered in this chapter.

Appreciating revivalism, but moving beyond its influence will require intentional teaching of its history. But without an exploration of revivalism's story and how it has shaped Evangelicals, efforts to renew worship within this tradition will be limited. As in any area of worship renewal, pastoral leadership is essential. The lead pastor must take the point because he or she is perceived as the primary worship leader of the church. Having served both as worship pastor and lead pastor, I speak from experience. As an associate pastor of worship, I could never lead the church beyond the understanding and practice of the lead pastor.

The last quarter of the twentieth century brought a movement in worship that would be both controversial and a God-send in that it would raise awareness of congregational worship in revivalist churches. The genesis of the Praise and Worship Movement is the topic of our next portrait.

Questions for Reflection:
1. Do you perceive revivalistic influences in the worship of your congregation? In what specific ways?

2. What does your congregation believe is the first priority of the church?
3. What does your congregation believe is the overall purpose of corporate worship?

4. What role do you think corporate worship plays in spiritual formation?

5. What is the role of music in your church's corporate worship? Is it limited to preparing the hearts of people to hear the sermon, or does it have its own worth?

6. Does your congregation participate as performers in worship or do they see themselves more as audience?

Suggested Reading:
Findlay, James F., *Dwight L. Moody: American Evangelist,* (Eugene, OR: Wipf & Stock Publishers, 1969, 2007).
Hustad, Donald P., *Jubilate II: Church Music in the Evangelical Tradition,* (Carol Stream, IL: Hope Publishing Company, 1993).

Kilde, Jeanne Halgren, *When Church Became Theatre: The Transformation of Evangelical Architecture and Worship in Nineteenth-Century America,* (New York: Oxford University Press, 2002).

McLaughlin, Jr., William L., *Modern Revivalism: Charles Grandison Finney to Billy Graham,* (Eugene, OR: Wipf & Stock Publishers, 1959, 2004).

Towns, Elmer L. and Whaley, Vernon M., *Worship Through the Ages,* (Nashville: B & H Publishing Group, 2012).

The Jesus People Movement

And it's very plain to see
It's not the way it used to be…
                    "Little Country Church"
                    Chuck Girard and Fred Field, 1971

Forest Home is a Christian conference center in the San Bernardino Mountains northeast of Los Angeles. It was founded in 1937 by Henrietta Mears, the dynamic Christian Education Director of Hollywood Presbyterian Church. Through the years, the center has had a profound impact on many American evangelical leaders. It was at Forest Home in 1949 that Billy Graham wrestled through rising doubts and became determined to press on in pursuing his evangelistic calling. Years later, in 1970, I too, encountered God in a powerful revival that swept through the camp.

I was raised in a very conservative Baptist home. Fundamentalism is my spiritual root-stock. I'm grateful for the solid foundation of biblical knowledge that it cultivated in me. But as the turmoil of the sixties wore on, tension began to rise in our home, as our pastor would repeatedly rail on the younger generation, including my older brother, who wasn't engaging in any kind of rebellious behavior at all. We finally decided to try out the so-called "liberal" American Baptist church in town. We had been warned that they were sponsoring teenage dances in the church basement, but we could no longer tolerate the negativism and legalism that we were experiencing in our home church. Much to our surprise, the pastor was evangelical and the people were quite welcoming. The youth group was vibrant and they laughed at our question about "dances" in the basement. We never went back to our fundamentalist church and roots.

Nine girls and I, along with the senior pastor, attended high school youth camp that summer at Forest Home. Pastor Ted Cole from First Baptist, Pomona, was the speaker for the week. As I recall, it started out as a typical youth camp. We met in the morning for devotions and an inspirational service. We sang the usual songs of the day, "How Great Thou Art" and Ralph Carmichael's "He's Everything to Me." Later in the morning, classes were offered for a variety of interests and there were many recreational choices in the afternoon. We gathered in the evening after dinner for an even more spiritually intense service and message. I do not recall the subject of Dr. Cole's messages. I do remember that by Tuesday night students were responding in significant numbers to the promptings of the Holy Spirit. Something unusual was happening.

Something unusual was happening. By Wednesday night, it seemed as if all heaven broke loose.

By Wednesday night, it seemed all heaven broke loose. Dr. Cole could not even complete his message; weeping and crying overwhelmed the place. He wisely dismissed us to be in solitude and do business with God. We would reconvene later at "Victory Circle."

Since the time of my conversion at age six until my experience at Forest Home, I always attended Sunday School and did the things a good Baptist boy should do. But in junior high, I cultivated a rich vocabulary that would have "made sailors blush" and mortified my parents. I had felt called to vocational ministry when I was eight years old, but in seventh grade, I investigated teaching rather than ministry to fulfill an assignment designed to promote reflection on possible future careers. I played the Christian game but I had no power. As I knelt by the huge rock at Forest Home, as Evangelicals often say, I gave my life completely to God again.[1]

---

[1] Such a "rededication experience" is not unusual for those who were converted as children. In fact, I believe it is necessary either as an event or process if the person is to mature as a Christian disciple. It is a "simple" act

118

It was the tradition of the camp to gather in the amphitheater on the closing night to share testimonies around a huge bonfire. Wednesday night was not the closing, but this week was clearly different. To their credit, the camp leaders realized God's schedule did not match their own. We started at 9:00 p.m. and could have gone longer but the leaders closed the gathering before midnight. Tears flowed as students publicly confessed their sins and reconciled with God and others. There was a steady stream of people ready to testify until the evening was closed. For the next two days, we would experience more of the same.

We arrived home on Saturday. The Sunday evening service was given over to the students to share our reflections, as was typical after summer camp. Most camp reflections that I have heard usually revolve around the fun activities students have had with a sprinkling of spiritual impact. Our reflection was the reverse. We were all given a chance to speak and each one of us told of the spiritual adventure we had taken together. What we had experienced at Forest Home spilled over to the old sanctuary at First Baptist, Oxnard that night. After the sharing was over and closing comments were being made, I felt an overwhelming compulsion to rise and challenge the congregation to love and repentance. The irresistible power of the Holy Spirit was poured out on us that night. Several people responded to an invitation, including my older brother, who had been jaded towards anything spiritual by the put-downs of our previous pastor. That night was the moment of his genuine conversion.

Unlike most typical camp experiences, however, the "afterglow" did not diminish when we came home. It seemed to gain momentum. During those years, I witnessed boldly and freely and found many who were receptive to the gospel. A number of students in our youth group started a before-school prayer meeting. Bible studies on campus were very common in public high schools. Students were outspoken about their faith. On college campuses, free speech platforms that had been the

---

(not to be disparaged) for a child to give his/her heart to Jesus. Their life is simple as is the choice for them. But as life gets more complex and full, the "simple" faith of the child must mature to match the circumstances and challenges of adolescence and adulthood.

venue for anti-war protests became the pulpits for student preachers proclaiming the gospel. In my own experience, openness to the gospel and dynamic vibrancy in the youth group lasted from 1969 to 1974.

Musical "Prophets"

When I returned from Forest Home, I had no idea that what I had experienced was part of a greater movement among teenagers and young adults. The Jesus People Movement would eventually impact the entire nation, but its vortex was in Southern California in 1969. After my experience at camp, I became aware of more happenings in L.A. My brother and I attended our first Christian music festival at the Hollywood Palladium in 1970. We had heard about the event through a street paper published by Duane Peterson called *The Hollywood Free Paper*. At the festival we heard music by Larry Norman, Ron Salisbury and the J.C. Power Outlet, Harvest Flight, and many others. Pat Boone and his daughters made a special appearance. After hours of hearing Christian bands and solo artists, evangelist Arthur Blessitt brought a short message and gave the invitation. Hundreds responded. A year later, we would attend a similar festival at the Hollywood Bowl. My brother bought Larry Norman's groundbreaking album published by Capital Records, *Upon This Rock*. We picked up our guitars and started singing "Sweet, Sweet Song of Salvation" and "I Wish We'd All Been Ready."

> *In sharp contrast to the earlier revivalism of the nineteenth and twentieth centuries, music was the main attraction, while the preacher played a supportive role.*

The Jesus People Movement was very closely identified with its music. Contemporary Christian Music (CCM) is one of its most lasting legacies. For the first several years, most of the songs written and sung by the artists were testimonial, birthed out of a strong evangelistic impulse. The Jesus People festivals were loosely modeled after their secular counterparts like Woodstock. In sharp contrast to the earlier revivalism of the nineteenth and twentieth centuries, music was the main attraction, while the preacher played a supportive role. At the festivals, the audience would listen to about three hours of evangelistic folk and rock songs. The preacher would then speak for only ten to fifteen minutes and give an altar call. The evangelistic effectiveness of the festival format was a harbinger of a very significant paradigm shift that would occur in evangelical churches in the coming years.

The shift is very easy to trace within the Baby Boomer generation. Boomers grew up during an era when the recording industry was coming of age. New recording technology and techniques along with growth in the number of rock and roll groups caused a cultural explosion of pop music. The turmoil of the '60's had provided ample material for anti-establishment young artists to write and produce protest songs. Music has always had a voice in cultural dissent. But with the growth of the broadcast industry in radio, TV, and recording, pop music claimed a powerful *prophetic* voice with the young. Many of the protest songs, of course, addressed the Vietnam War. There were, however, many other counter-cultural impulses that the young artists promoted, including drug use, "free love," anti-capitalism, and racial reconciliation. It was not surprising then that music would take the primary *prophetic* role for Boomers in order to proclaim the counter-cultural good news of the gospel. An important legacy of the Jesus People Movement was that music was leveraged as the primary vehicle for mass evangelism. For these young Evangelicals, music would no longer be relegated to the revivalist utilitarian role of "preparing the hearts of the people to hear God's Word." This change would be a significant paradigm shift for the church. After the Jesus People Movement, *music in worship would hold its own intrinsic value.*

Calvary Chapel's Concerts and Stable of Musicians

In the Orange County town of Costa Mesa, Chuck Smith's little church, Calvary Chapel, was experiencing explosive growth with an influx of converted hippies and surf bums. Smith possessed a warm, fatherly manner and a slow, deliberate style of preaching the Bible that was very attractive to the new Christians. Unlike most evangelical pastors at the time who were put off by the youthful, rebellious symbols of long hair, bare feet, and blue jeans in church, Chuck Smith welcomed them into his congregation. In describing the growth of Calvary Chapel during the 1970's, Smith would later reflect:

> Scholars such as Peter Wagner (Fuller Theological Seminary) and Ron Enroth (Westmont College) have observed this phenomenon and noted that it is not likely anything of such colossal proportions has occurred in American history. One estimate put the total number of Calvary Chapel (Costa Mesa) baptisms performed over a two-year period during the mid-1970's at well over 8,000. Additionally, over 20,000 conversions to the Christian faith took place during that same period. According to church growth experts, Calvary Chapel's 10-year growth rate was almost 10,000 percent![2]

Early on, Calvary Chapel's music consisted of traditional gospel songs and hymns. But several of the young Christians were accomplished musicians and began to write songs about their new-found faith. Musical groups such as *Children of the Day, Love Song,* and *Country Faith,* along with solo artists like Karen Lafferty and Debbie Kerner, were gaining a growing audience. Smith encouraged them and provided the church as a venue for them to give evangelistic concerts on Saturday nights. The Saturday night concerts proved to be very popular well into the 1970's. By 1972, the bands were touring extensively, giving evangelistic concerts around the region and spreading their Jesus People message.

In 1971, Pastor Chuck Smith established Maranatha! Music to support Calvary Chapel's growing music ministry.[3] Their first

---

[2] Chuck Smith, *The History of Calvary Chapel,* (Costa Mesa, CA, The Word for Today) as quoted by Bill Jackson in *The Quest for the Radical Middle* (Cape Town, South Africa: Vineyard International Publishing, 1999), p. 37.

[3] An album discography from 1971-1989 for Maranatha! Music can be found at

album, *The Everlastin' Living Jesus Concert,* was a successful groundbreaking venture for several of Calvary's best groups. The recording and those that would follow pushed the popularity of the bands and musical artists far beyond the Southern California region. Like the music in the Jesus People Festivals of L.A. a few years before, most of the music being written and sung by the early Maranatha! Music musicians was testimonial and evangelistic in nature. But as Calvary Chapel continued to grow from the influx of young Christians, new worship music was needed to resonate with them. Calvary's musicians naturally responded and began to write simple songs – mostly in a folk idiom – for use in corporate worship. Songs like *Praise the Lord, Seek Ye First,* and *Father, I Adore You* were typical of the worship songs being written in the early 1970's. *Praise* was released by Maranatha! Music in 1974. It was the first of nine *Praise* albums that would effectively promote the early music of praise and worship around the country and eventually the world. Maranatha! also produced compilations of their songs in thick spiral-bound books to enable

**The Everlastin'
Living Jesus Concert**

Chuck Girard & Love Song
Little Country Church

Selah
In Jesus' Name

Blessed Hope
Something More

Country Faith
Two Roads

Combined Groups
Holy, Holy, Holy

Gentle Faith
The Shepherd

Debbie Kerner
Behold, I Stand at the Door

The Way
If You Will Believe

Chuck Girard & Love Song
Maranatha

Children of the Day
For Those Tears I Died

< http://www.bsnpubs.com/word/maranatha/maranatha.html>
Accessed July 16, 2014.

churches to sing the music. Long before the *Praise Album* was recorded, the Jesus People Movement had grown beyond a counter-cultural phenomenon in the California hippie culture to draw in young people like me from established traditional churches. It was becoming "mainstream." Overhead projectors splashing song lyrics on the wall in a trademark "keystone" image became more and more of a fixture in evangelical churches trying to integrate young people and the new worship music into their services.

Praise and Worship Music Becomes a Movement

Aside from the resistance that traditional church members felt about the music, purveyors of the new style of worship music faced a daunting problem. Most of them were illegally projecting and distributing the songs. Under the law, it is illegal to duplicate or project the lyrics of a copyrighted song for people to sing without permission from the copyright owner. With the proliferation of the songs and the burgeoning desire to use them, it was virtually impossible for churches to contact each of the publishers to ask permission to use them and pay the royalties required. The cost was prohibitive and the administrative burden unbearable. I will always remember my encounter with the new church secretary where I was the minister of music who insisted that I secure permission to use each of the songs or she would not put them into the bulletin. If I refused, she would resign. Of course, she was ethically right and I was wrong. But I was handcuffed by the overwhelming administrative logistics required and I was doing what 99% percent of all the other church musicians were doing.

About the same time that I had the encounter with my principled secretary, a needed solution presented itself. In 1988, Howard Rachinski, who was also a minister of music facing the same dilemma, launched Christian Copyright Licensing, International (CCLI) to address the issue. CCLI allowed a church to pay an annual fee, set according to the size of the ministry, to cover copyright use for the publishers the company represented. Recognizing the value and ease of such an arrangement, most

Christian publishing companies soon aligned with CCLI. The advent of CCLI propelled the explosion of praise and worship music into its own movement by the late 1980's.

The other development that aided in the explosion of praise and worship music was the emergence of Integrity's Hosanna! Music. Like Chuck Smith's Maranatha! Music, Hosanna!'s start was "organic" and grew out of an already existing ministry. Keyboardist Tom Brooks had studio experience with audio production and got the idea to record a live worship service at his church, Grace World Outreach, in St. Louis, in 1983. They duplicated the project onto cassette tapes and distributed it for people within the church's sphere of influence. The publishers of *New Wine Magazine* happened to hear the recording and asked if they could run an advertisement promoting the project. Sales of the first cassette, *Behold His Majesty*, were far beyond expectations. *New Wine* wanted to promote another recording for their next issue and Brooks was agreeable. *Let Praise Arise* did even better. The magazine, which was already in decline, folded their operation a few issues later but offered worship musicians the

> **The advent of CCLI propelled the explosion of praise and worship music into a movement by the late 1980's.**

opportunity to take over the rhythm of their eight-week publication as a subscription series to a worship recording. The enterprise was a fabulous success and Hosanna! Music was born.

Maranatha! Music produced their *Praise* albums as compilations. Calvary Chapel's ecclesiastical cousin, The Vineyard,[4] began to publish and distribute their worship music in

---

[4] Chuck Smith was uncomfortable with John Wimber's journey into "signs and wonders" at Calvary Chapel, Yorba Linda where he was the senior pastor. Wimber's church eventually aligned with the Association of Vineyard Churches, led by Kenn Gullicksen in 1982. Wimber's gifts and experience in church growth quickly made him the primary leader of the Vineyard churches. (Bill Jackson, *The Quest for the Radical Middle*, Cape Town, South Africa: Vineyard International Publishing, 1999) p. 85-86.

1983 on cassettes. Hosanna! Music, however, holds a distinctive place of importance in the growth of the Praise and Worship Movement in at least two ways. First, they were very aggressive in their marketing. I remember receiving a recording in the mail from them without requesting it and without obligation. If I liked it, all I needed to do was to return the card with payment for the first recording and I would be put on the subscription list. If I didn't like it, I could keep the recording as a gift. The strategy worked on me and countless others. Hosanna! quickly provided churches with a lot of new music through their distribution of a new project every other month. Along with the recording, Hosanna! would also include a song book, complete with musical notation, chords, and lyrics. The productions were big (it was the '80's, after all) and quality was good. I looked forward to each new installment. Hosanna!'s marketing and business plan was very instrumental and effective in the spread of new worship music.

Besides their effective marketing strategy, Hosanna! brought another important ingredient onto the landscape of the fledgling Praise and Worship Movement. Unlike hymns, praise and worship songs are usually sung in medleys called "sets." The sets for the Hosanna! projects were typically forty minutes long and would take the worshippers on a progressive spiritual journey of praise and adoration. The theological and musical flow of the projects was sensitive and sophisticated. In the early years of my ministry, I learned a lot from their recordings and music booklets. The ministries featured on Hosanna!'s projects were not the only ones who would take worshippers on a progressive spiritual journey in music, but because their distribution was so wide, they were probably the most influential. Most churches that do contemporary praise and worship music in their services combine songs together into a set rather than stand-alone songs, which were typical of the hymn tradition.

The Emergence of Worship Wars

By the mid-1980's most evangelical churches that were growing utilized contemporary praise music to some extent. Boomers were becoming very influential in church leadership and many who had left the faith after childhood were returning because they had settled down to raise their own families. There was a Boomer "Boomerang" back to church because new parents wanted their children to have some level of faith background. Churches that spoke the musical language of the Boomers reaped the benefit of their return. Church growth gurus insisted that the new music was absolutely essential and many pastors willingly followed the plan. While new-paradigm churches like Calvary Chapel and the Vineyard had no problems incorporating praise and worship music into their services (most used it exclusively), traditional, established churches found the change in music very difficult.[5]

During that time, many in the Builder generation (the parents of Boomers) were still alive and influential in established churches. To them, guitars and drums only reminded them of the rebellion that they had had to endure raising their teenagers. And besides, there were plenty of voices boldly declaring that rock and roll was Satanic and because of that, guitars and drums should be anathema in the church. In addition, the ears of many older people become sensitive to loud sounds and the

> *To [Builders], guitars and drums only reminded them of the rebellion that they had to endure raising their teenagers.*

bands playing the new music tended to be louder than the piano and organ that seniors were used to. The frequent repetitions found in contemporary praise and worship made no sense to them. Older people not only struggled with the change to a new style of music, but they also understandably grieved the loss of the hymns and songs that had shaped their spiritual lives. All of these factors made many older Christians quite averse to the new church music.

The outcome of the worship wars was both tragic and transformational. Churches split over the debate about musical styles. Many languished or died because they refused to update

---

[5] At Chuck Smith's Calvary Chapel, morning service was relatively traditional, incorporating hymns. Sunday night services, Saturday night concerts, and small home groups used the fresh contemporary songs.

their ministry while others were destroyed by bully pastors imposing their will rather than exercising godly patience. Many churches split within themselves, offering different services based on style preference and, in effect, forming separate congregations. But all the while we were arguing over music and worship style, a massive paradigm shift was taking place within the evangelical church. Prior to 1980, one would have had a hard time finding any books on the topic of worship written by evangelical writers. There were less than a handful. Today, there are hundreds. Interest in worship among Evangelicals has never been higher. The emergence of the Praise and Worship Movement and the rising tensions that it brought cultivated a deep interest in the topic of worship throughout the evangelical church.

The Nature of Praise and Worship Music

Contemporary praise and worship music has become a fixture in evangelical churches. There is no turning back the tide. It is here to stay. But the form and understanding of the genre has "run off the tracks" in many places. What the Jesus People experienced in their worship gatherings is often far from what a worshipper in a typical evangelical church in America might experience forty years later. I recall in the mid-1980's attending a number of church growth conferences where the facilitators – who seemingly had no experience or expertise in worship theology – told their audiences that praise and worship music must be embraced in order for their church to grow. Frequently, the music was adopted and embraced without the ethos that was present in the early days of Calvary Chapel and the Vineyard. I believe the disconnect was a contributing factor to the worship wars.

In their corporate worship, the early Jesus People were experiencing a whole new dynamic as they sang <u>to</u> God rather than just <u>about</u> God. Through their new, simple music, the evangelical church was waking up to engaging with God in worship. Unlike the revivalists before them, music for the Jesus People was not just a warm-up to "prepare the hearts of the people" for the preacher. *Music had its own worth as a conduit of engagement with God in worship.* Practitioners, theologians, and historians would later identify this quality as a *sacrament*.[6] In my mind, contemporary praise music as a sacrament is the great gift and paradigm shift that happened in evangelical corporate worship and is a legacy of the movement. People actually began to connect with God through their singing. It would be

> *Music had its own worth as a conduit of engagement with God in worship.*

arrogant to assert that this kind of worship had never happened before. It certainly had. A.W. Tozer spoke of deep spiritual engagement as he sang classic hymns.[7] But after several generations of Evangelicals on a full diet of testimony gospel songs, the new "praise choruses" ushered in a whole new understanding and experience in worship.

Jesus People were not ashamed to express publicly how they felt about God. The movement was an environment in which people were not afraid of the mysterious work of God and were willing to take a risk to experience more of him in their lives. The hunger and desire for genuine connection with God through music is at the heart of the Praise and Worship Movement. Every description of Jesus People worship illustrates their passion to connect with him. The closed eyes, the raised hands, the tears, were all manifestations of people who unashamedly were seeking a divine encounter. Worshipping through contemporary praise and worship music is, in a sense, a transcendent and mystical experience. And it is, almost always, an emotional experience.

---

[6] Robert Webber commented several times at The Institute for Worship Studies that Chuck Fromm, founder of *Worship Leader Magazine*, considered praise and worship music to be a "new sacrament." Worship historians Swee Hong Lim and Lester Ruth affirm and develop the concept further in their book, *Loving on Jesus: A Concise History of Contemporary Worship* (2017).

[7] Ron Eggert, ed. *Tozer on Christian Leadership: A 366-Day Devotional,* (Camp Hill, PA: Wing Spread Publishers, 2001), June 3.

One cannot sing praise and worship songs the same way that gospel hymns were sung – "to prepare hearts to hear the sermon." The one who sings praise and worship songs with the same expectations that he sings hymns will be disappointed. Generally, hymns express compact theological truths through profound and beautiful poetry. While they engage the emotions, their primary value is in the substance of their text; they engage the intellect. Most praise and worship songs, on the other hand, express a theological concept simply, but in a deeply emotional way. They engage the affections. Admittedly, such a distinction between traditional hymns and praise and worship songs is simplistic.

In order to understand and engage with God through praise and worship music, the worshipper needs to be willing to release his or her emotions into the song.

There are hymns that are very emotional – many of the Lutheran chorales come to mind. And there are praise and worship songs that have deep theology – "Remembrance" by Matt Maher and Matt Redman is an excellent example, exploring the mystery of the Eucharist. But the distinction of praise and worship songs being necessarily emotional is an important one to make for this discussion.

In our modern world, we are prone to exalt reason over emotion. You see it everywhere in our culture – even our Christian culture. It is acceptable to demean and marginalize our emotions. But such a divide between intellect and emotion is unfortunate and unnecessary. It is definitely not biblical. Read the psalms. They are drenched with emotion. We are to love the Lord with all our heart, soul, and strength (Deut. 6:8). Praise and worship songs can help to give voice to our emotions and affections toward God. That is why people in praise and worship cultures lift their hands, close their eyes, and are not afraid of tears. Some of them even jump around and dance! In order to understand and engage with God through praise and worship music, the worshipper needs to be willing to release his or her emotions into the song. They have to engage emotionally, to enter into the affect or feeling of the song.[8]

The Jesus People Movement is closely associated with the Charismatic Movement. While Chuck Smith allowed, but moderated, the practice of supernatural spiritual gifts like healing and speaking in tongues, John Wimber and the Vineyard churches celebrated them. Grace World Outreach in St. Louis, where Hosanna! Music was birthed, was Charismatic as well. Nearly every ministry where contemporary praise and worship was being generated at the beginning of the movement had some level of Charismatic influence. It is not surprising, then, that many non-Charismatics find it difficult to understand and embrace the kind of transcendent experience in singing that the Jesus People knew. Charismatics, by nature, tend to be emotionally vulnerable. Entering into the affect of a worship song comes very naturally to them and it remains one of the unique powerful qualities of praise and worship music.

This vulnerability – this nakedness of soul – is a prerequisite for the worshipper who seeks to engage with God through these simple praise and worship songs. It is one of the reasons why freedom of physical expression is a mark of this kind of worship. People who will not risk the loss of their dignity through vulnerable actions will likely never fully experience the richness of worship that praise and worship offers.

That is a lot to ask of non-Charismatics. For contemporary praise and worship music to resonate genuinely with the worshipper, there must be a commitment to the song – entering into its message and dwelling there. This is not idolatry of the song. Such a commitment – a giving of oneself – is meditation and contemplation of God's holy character and works. It is why

---

[8] The idea of emotional engagement in music is not new, of course. Music in certain classical eras, such as the Romantic and Baroque periods, required it. Music in the Baroque period, in particular, expressed a specific "affect" in each piece. Each movement in Handel's *Messiah*, for example, requires engagement of a singular, or in some arias, two affects. Good performance practice requires emotional commitment. Though much less sophisticated, I suggest that praise and worship songs are similar in this regard.

so many contemporary songs repeat over and over again. For the one who has "entered into the song," that is not a problem at all. For those who cannot release themselves into the song, repetition is annoying because it is not meaningful.

Still, non-Charismatics should be encouraged to grow in their emotional vulnerability. Biblical physical engagement such as lifting hands can be very helpful in releasing the emotional reserve of worshippers. The early days of the Charismatic Movement were very divisive, cultivating a great amount of fear among many Evangelicals. For the most part, the fear has abated. Lifting your hands in worship, moving your feet just a bit, or shedding a tear doesn't make one a Charismatic. But those actions can be manifestations of a more fully-orbed and biblical worship experience. Far beyond the relevance of the folk-rock style of praise and worship music, that is the great gift of the movement.

Problems with the Praise & Worship Movement

Contemporary praise and worship music, with all of its significant benefit in emotional engagement and cultural relevance, has a number of challenges and pitfalls. Wise pastors and worship leaders will guide their congregations through these potentially dangerous tendencies and practical difficulties.

There is a sense among many in ministry leadership today that congregational singing is in demise. That may be so. Historically, there has always been an ebb and flow in the vitality of church music. Critics of the praise and worship genre would pin the blame for the demise of hymn-singing on the growth of "praise choruses." There may be something to that criticism, to be honest. Hymn singing in the last two hundred years was generally supported by an organ – a wind instrument that sustains pitches much like the human voice. Praise and worship music has no such vocal support from the instruments. Instead, vocal support for the congregation comes from singers amplified by microphones.

The demise of the hymnal is also problematic. With hymn singing, the people in the congregation could have the music in front of them and even if the singer couldn't read music, they could tell if the pitch in the melody was going up or down.

Furthermore, able musicians in the congregation were able to read and sing in four-part harmony. (That's how I learned to read bass clef.) The loss of congregational four-part harmony is real with the emergence of praise music. A hymnal also provides the opportunity for the worshipper to linger with a text if a phrase or word resonates in his or her spirit. The incessant progression of song slides provides no such opportunity for textual contemplation. (I confess that a favorite practice of mine when I was younger and oblivious to my rudeness was to explore the hymnal when the sermon was boring. Not really such a bad option.) Finally, hymnals have long served alongside of the Bible as a wonderful aid to personal devotion. That is certainly my testimony. With the disappearance of hymnals from our churches, we are losing something very significant. I, along with many others, grieve the loss.

But the demise of congregational singing should not be laid entirely at the feet of the new musical genre. The fault, I believe, lies squarely on the shoulders of unreflective musical leadership that disempowers congregational singing. Worship leaders need to understand their role in leading the congregation in musical worship. Too often, the leader's concern is in producing a certain sound with the band rather than engaging the people. There are many things that will cause a congregation to stop singing.

Worship leaders and sound technicians need to be aware that if members of the congregation cannot hear their own voice singing, most will stop and just listen. The band may be musically excellent and the songs eminently sing-able, but if the sound is too loud, most people will disengage. In order to sing and tune one's voice to another (the essence of congregational singing) the singer needs to hear his own voice. There is, of course, a balance here. If all one hears is his own voice, as in an acoustically dead room, most will stop singing, unless, of course, they are confident soloists who like to show off a bit. But if a worshipper can hear his voice blending with others, the effect is inviting and pleasing. Each venue and each congregation is different. What may be too loud on the decibel meter in one place may be just fine in another. I have observed, unfortunately, when I've raised this topic with some leaders, they've ignored my concerns, only to have their people disengaged. I understand the desire for energy produced by loud music. I, too, enjoy the feel of sub-woofers thumping on my chest. But leaders should be careful to consider the effect of too much sound and monitor their congregation closely. If they are not singing, perhaps the volume is too high.

Another reason why singers may disengage is because the song is in the wrong key (too high or too low) or the range is too wide. Chris Tomlin's songs, which are generally very sing-able, usually need to be keyed down a minor third in order for most people to be able to sing the notes. Also, leaders should be very careful not to press the range of a song much beyond an octave. There are, of course, exceptions. *In Christ Alone*, by Stuart Townend and Keith Getty, is very sing-able and regarded as one of the best songs in the last twenty years. Nevertheless, it has a range of an octave and a fourth. There are many exceptions, but leaders need to be discerning about sing-ability.

Another musical characteristic of praise and worship songs that may present a challenge is the employment of syncopation. Church music scholar Bert Polman recommends straightening out some of the rhythms.[9] Unfortunately, such rhythmic alteration destroys the song, in my opinion, but for some congregations, such alteration may be the only way to do a particular song. Worship leaders must know their people. If the congregation is younger and many of the members listen to praise and worship songs, they may be quite capable of executing sophisticated syncopations. Unlike hymns and choral music, praise and worship music is learned more by ear than off the page. But if a congregation struggles with syncopation, leaders should moderate their use of it.[10] If the song is too syncopated for the congregation and the leader insists on using it, it can be sung by a soloist or

---

[9] Bert Polman, "Praise the Name of Jesus" in *The Message in the Music,* ed. By Robert Woods and Brian Walrath (Nashville: Abingdon Press, 2007) p. 133.

[10] I have found syncopation to be a problem with many liturgical and traditional churches in the upper Midwest who have a strong hymn and choral tradition (Reformed and Lutheran, in particular). Syncopation is not a usual part of their musical vocabulary and congregations tend to "straighten out" the rhythms naturally.

ensemble. Better to listen for a verse or two than to be totally frustrated by the whole song.

Recently, worship leaders have begun assigning leadership of particular songs or verses to a soloist in the praise team. I believe the practice is a good one, varying the sound and providing a diversity of leadership. I have observed, however, that an unfortunate effect of this shared leadership is confusion in the congregation. Congregations need to be encouraged to sing even when a soloist is leading. The problem can be ironically compounded if the soloist has an exceptional voice. The congregation may prefer to hear the soloist and passively listen. The remedy is for each person on the praise team to understand their role in engaging the congregation in singing. Each leader should always monitor the level of engagement of the congregation and when it diminishes, they should encourage the congregation to join in.

Beyond these practical concerns, there are intrinsic problems with contemporary praise and worship music as a genre. In the early 2000's, the focus of a number of CCM artists, exemplified perhaps most significantly by Michael W. Smith, changed from testimonial songs to worship. The shift was by no means across the board in repertoire focus or in its effect for popular bands, but its impact was to establish a new kind of professional musician, "the worship artist." The intent, from the artists' perspective, was to express their deepest motivations and love for God. They did not wish to be viewed simply as a popular artist, but rather first as a committed follower and lover of Christ. Within just a few years, there were more and more artists and bands deemed exclusively "worship artists." The positive effect was to spread the worship impulse and songs even deeper and further across the evangelical landscape.

The unintended negative consequence was the formation of a "worship-industrial complex" that included not only performing musicians but also their agents, publishers, distributers, and radio station managers.[11] Assuming the best, that all of the people

---

[11] Harold Best explores the challenges brought about by these "gatekeepers" of electronic media in *Music Through the Eyes of Faith,* (New York: HarperCollins Publishers, 1993), p. 160-161.

involved are seeking to do God's work in the Kingdom, the unfortunate reality is that material profit and growth become factors in determining what kind of music gets written, recorded, and promoted. To consider even the smallest amount of capitalistic motivation as one of the "gate-keepers" in determining the worship song repertoire of our churches is disturbing. Discerning church leaders will consider that reality when choosing their worship song diet.

Another negative consequence of the emergence of "the worship-industrial complex" is that musicians leading worship in the local church began to mimic the same performance techniques of the "worship artists." As is the case in the secular world, Christians are prone to idolizing popular artists. Nothing could be more repulsive to God (and I would think the artists, themselves) than to steal glory that is due him and give it to the performer. And we are often naïve, unreflectively using the techniques of the world to highlight the artist and promote a performance culture in worship. When I was teaching worship leadership at Huntington University from 2005 to 2010, I endeavored to help aspiring leaders to understand the self-defeating techniques that were being used in their venue which actually undermined corporate participation. The technical director insisted on using concert lighting effects for the worship gatherings. Focused and moving lights along with fog machines, drew attention to the band, which received enthusiastic applause but tepid singing from the students. The house lights were always dim, diminishing any sense of corporate identity and promoting an intensely private experience. Moreover, the worship leaders could not see the student body and gauge their level of worship involvement.

There may be a place for stage lights and fog machines in worship, but they must be used to draw us to God rather than to the platform. Dimmed house lighting is standard for concerts and it is very difficult to redirect an experienced technical director to raise them. His role, after all, is an artistic one, applying his knowledge and expertise to make the "stage" attractively compelling. But corporate worship is a very different dynamic than a concert. Brighter house lighting enforces a *corporate identity*, which is essential for the church to worship biblically. House lights may be dimmed effectively at times if the worship set leads to a contemplative moment. But continually dimmed house lights with a lit platform should be generally avoided because it promotes a "performance" or "concert" ethos.

It is very easy in praise and worship to draw attention to oneself on the platform. It goes with popular musical culture. But the focus of attention in worship must obviously be on God rather than the musicians. *The burden of the worship leader is to lead the people in engaging with God through music.* I have observed many young and inexperienced leaders who do not understand their role as worship facilitators for the congregation. In their enthusiasm for learning their musical craft, they are not aware of the sacred duty with which they've been entrusted. While such a problem may be observed with older worship musicians, it is a developmental passage that seems to affect many younger ones. It makes sense. The thrill of continually learning new musical skills and performing them in public is intoxicating. Mature leadership is required to help them become leaders who are servants of the congregation rather than self-promoters showing off their skills – even if subconsciously - in a worship setting.

> ***The burden of the worship leader is to lead the people in engaging with God through music.***

A second intrinsic problem with contemporary praise and worship is its tendency to reflect the cultural values of the world in the content of the text. The self-focus of contemporary American culture has already been noted in the chapter on Pietism, and its presence is so pervasive within evangelical churches that it is very difficult to root out without raising eyebrows. Contemporary praise and worship, much more than the hymn tradition, has been prone to promoting therapeutic worship songs, certainly since the 1990's. Self-focused worship songs are the result of immature theological reflection within a narcissistic culture. Fortunately, the trend in worship song writing since the early years of the new century has been toward more thoughtful theological reflection. While Evangelicals will always have a large repertoire of personal worship songs (our emphasis is on "a personal relationship with Christ"), there are now a greater number of songs written for the congregation utilizing plural pronouns. Robert Webber's critique of "I-Me-My Songs" in *Worship Leader Magazine,* along with many other voices, has no doubt caused some song writers to reduce the self-focus in their output.[12]

Finally, because praise and worship music is, by nature, emotionally engaging, it is subject to emotional manipulation. There is an unstated but understood expectation that worship music should elicit a deep emotional response each week. High emotional intensity is impossible to maintain each week. It should not be our intention to do so. We are idolaters, worshipping the experience rather than God when we subject ourselves to this "tyranny of the sincere."[13] This is a great danger, and pastors and worship leaders need to be aware of this negative potential. It is very easy to shape musical technique to move people emotionally. Build it up here; break it down there. Musicians have intuitive formulas for conjuring affective responses. When that happens, worship is being empowered by manipulation and emotion rather than the Holy Spirit. On the other hand, the impulses of the Spirit often come as a delightful surprise. Worship leaders should provide space in their planning for these spontaneous leadings and learn to discern them. Pastors and leaders must take care to be sure that it is the Spirit that empowers our affections rather than the music manipulating us to shallow and meaningless "worship."

What is driving the train in the emotion-laden song sets of contemporary praise and worship? The answer to that question can be very challenging to discern. If the emotional patterns are

---

[12] Robert Webber, "I – Me – My Worship?" *Worship Leader* (January/February, 2005), 10.

[13] Kent Carlson and Mike Lueken, *Renovation of the Church: What Happens When a Seeker Church Discovers Spiritual Formation* (Downers Grove, IL: Intervarsity Press, 2011) p. 157.

similar from week to week, it is a good chance that they are being contrived and manipulated. If there is an overemphasis on stage lighting or constant use of the same musical techniques, it is likely that manipulation is in play. It is very tempting for a worship leader to choreograph every movement and feeling sub-consciously within a worship set. The truth is, there are many musical tools available to the able musician that will move the people. The effectiveness of a movie score is simple proof of the power of music to elicit emotion. The worship leader's role is to empower the worship voice of the people rather than drive it through manipulation. A leader who patiently and prayerfully serves his or her people will be the one that will not be seduced by the power of their music to manipulate.

Summary and Path for Renewal

The Jesus People Movement happened fifty years ago. Still, as I have written in this chapter, its memories remain fresh. I have contributed snapshots from my own experiences to this strategic family portrait. The challenge of researching recent church history, as one scholar has put it, is that the subjects of inquiry can actually talk back to you.[14] Still, recent history is instructive and inspirational to us in the same way that previous portraits in this study have provided insight. We can affirm with gratitude that God poured out his Spirit in revival through the Jesus People Movement. Reviewing the original intention and motivations of the early movement in contemporary praise and worship can serve as a corrective to deepen our practice and experience today.

Research and reflection into the Jesus People Movement and its offspring, the Praise and Worship Movement, is comparatively new. David DiSabatino, with his exhaustive bibliography, was the first to pursue the story seriously and remains an important chronicler.[15] The most thorough and reflective history of the Jesus People Movement to date is found in Larry Eskridge's *God's*

---

[14] A somewhat humorous comment made by Lester Ruth in a seminar at The Robert Webber Institute for Worship Studies, June 19, 2017.

[15] David DiSabatino, *The Jesus People Movement: An Annotated Bibliography and General Resource,* (City: Greenwood Press, 1999).

Forever Family.[16]   The focus in this chapter has been on understanding the roots of praise and worship music in the Jesus People and Charismatic Movements.

Praise and worship music has been nearly universally adopted at some level in evangelical churches. Some churches use it exclusively while others may use only a limited number of praise and worship songs within a traditional context. Many churches find themselves in the middle, using both traditional hymns and contemporary songs in a sometimes uneasy balance. This chapter seeks to explain the affective riches of praise and worship growing out of the passionate and expressive Jesus People and Charismatic Movements. It is, above all, an *experiential* music that is meant to engage an emotional chord in the worshipper. Unfortunately, many of the benefits of the worship style go unrealized because of the emotional reserve of worshippers. Those who use contemporary praise and worship music in their services should be encouraged to lessen their guard and make an "emotional commitment" to the songs.

Of course, with praise and worship music being a powerfully emotional genre, there are certain dangers that are inherent in the style which have been explored in this chapter. The path for renewal is to be found in the maturity of contemporary worship leaders. Contemporary music is, by nature, geared to the young, for whom the next big thing and "relevance" may hold the highest value. Mature leaders need to understand the dangers as explained in this chapter and be proactive in guiding musicians and the congregation away from them. Many of the seasoned worship leaders in the Praise and Worship Movement have written books or offer seminars in leadership which reflect the kind of mature discernment that is required.[17] Many of the Boomer and Gen X leaders who pioneered praise and worship in their settings should consider shifting their roles from exclusively leading worship to becoming effective mentors for younger worship leaders.

---

[16] Larry Eskridge, *God's Forever Family*, (New York: Oxford University Press, 2013).

[17] See the selected reading list for some suggestions.

Questions for Reflection:

1. What were your earliest experiences and impressions with praise and worship music?
2. Do you agree that contemporary praise and worship songs require an emotional investment? Why or why not?

3. Is your congregation physically expressive in worship? Do you believe it is an important element in contemporary praise and worship?
4. Have you dealt with any of the dangers of praise and worship discussed in the chapter? Which do you feel are the most dangerous for your congregation?

5. How can you get your congregation to be more emotionally engaged in worship? Do you think emotional engagement is important?

Suggested Reading: History of the Jesus People Movement:

DiSabatino, David, *The Jesus People Movement: An Annotated Bibliography and General Resource,* (Jester Media, 2003).

Eskridge, Larry, *God's Forever Family: The Jesus People Movement in America,* (New York: Oxford University Press, 2013).

Lim, Swee Hong and Ruth, Lester, *Lovin' on Jesus: A Concise History of Contemporary Worship,* (Nashville: Abingdon Press, 2017).

Pederson, Duane, *Jesus People*, (Ventura, CA: Gospel Light/Regal Books, 1971).

Suggested Reading: Praise and Worship Leadership:

Hayford, Jack, *Worship His Majesty,* (Dallas: Word Music, 1987).

Kauflin, Bob, *Worship Matters: Leading Others to Encounter the Greatness of God,* (Wheaton: Crossway Book, 2008).

Park, Andy, *To Know You More: Cultivating the Heart of the Worship Leader,* (Downers Grove: Intervarsity Press, 2002).

Park, Andy, Ruth, Lester, & Rethmeier, *Worshipping with the Anaheim Vineyard: The Emergence of Contemporary Worship,*

(Grand Rapids: William B. Eerdmans Publishing Company, 2003).

Plantinga, Jr., Cornelius & Rozeboom, Sue A., *Discerning the Spirits: A Guide to Thinking About Christian Worship Today,* (Grand Rapids: William B. Eerdmans Publishing Company, 2003).

Wimber, John, ed., *Thoughts on Worship,* (Anaheim: Vineyard Music Group, 1996).

Filtering the Waters
of Willow Creek

Too many people were observing the show but not meeting God. They meandered in and out of relationship but weren't in real community. They sought their spiritual fix but didn't give themselves fully to Christ.

Walt Kallestad,
Pastor of Community Church of Joy, Phoenix[1]

In 2010, I attended one of the satellite broadcasts of the *Willow Creek Association Global Leadership Summit.* The list of speakers was quite impressive and the substance of their presentations was thought-provoking. I can still recall Robert Reich's talk on altruistic motivation, China's economic minister speaking about the impact of Christianity on progressive Chinese culture, and the inspiring story of TOM's Shoes. I also remember the host's condescending remarks about traditional churches. As he welcomed everyone to the event, he admitted that some might be surprised to have such a world-class event hosted by a local church. "But not to worry," he said, "you won't have to sing old hymns or hear a bad choir here." I cringed. His comment

---

[1] Walt Kallestad and Jim Wilson, *"Showtime!" No More,* Christianity Today, Fall, 2008. http://www.christianitytoday.com/pastors/2008/fall/13.39.html. Accessed 1.25.2017.

illustrated the mindset of many seeker-driven churches against any and all traditions. I recognized Willow's bias because I had encountered it many years before when I served in my first full-time worship position in the late 1980s.

My path to full-time worship vocation was not direct. I had to wait for my opportunity. I had prepared myself to be a minister of music by enrolling at Biola University as a music major. My undergraduate journey was not without its challenges, but nevertheless, I did graduate with a B.A. in music and I expected to secure a full-time position in a church ministry. Into every young life some disillusionment must come and my failure to secure such an appointment hit pretty hard. But I was hired to be a music specialist at a Christian School serving K-8 students.

I could have never foreseen it, but my experience at the Christian School led me to take another position at a similar but much larger school which was a ministry of the church I attended while in high school. Even though I wasn't in full-time church music ministry, it was nice to come home. Shortly after I started, however, the minister of music was forced to resign and I was recruited to serve as the interim minister until a permanent one could be hired. My pathway had many twists and turns, but I was eventually offered the position two years later. My term as interim during a very difficult season in the church had purchased a good deal of trust and credibility for me to launch my first full-time position in my preferred vocation. It was my "dream job."

At Biola, I was well-immersed in hymnology and traditional church music. But as a product of the Jesus People Movement, I was also committed to the new praise and worship genre. With a wide appreciation of both, I've always tried to lead congregations to embrace a broad spectrum of worship music. I've also received a healthy dose of criticism. That included from the new Executive Pastor (XP) that the church had hired.

While I was on staff, we were well-positioned for substantial growth. Our facilities were more than adequate. Lowering of double-digit mortgage rates in the mid-1980s unleased a real estate explosion in the community. The church went from 400 attendees to nearly 1,000 in less than two years. The XP that was hired to accommodate our growth was influenced by the increasing impact of Willow Creek Church. The staff began attending church growth seminars that prescribed getting rid of all hymns and choirs and fully embracing the new contemporary praise and worship music style. While I was bothered by the callous disposal of church tradition and disregard for the people who struggled with such a shift, I was even more bothered by the fact that the church growth experts had never done any serious study and reflection on the topic of Christian worship. To them, just doing the right style of music was essential in order to get Boomers to come back to church. We had to provide the "worship product" and programming that appealed to them.

I wasn't on staff too long when I began to experience tension with the XP. I still wanted to include some hymns in the worship service, but he was determined to eliminate them. I was frustrated that he, like the church growth consultants, had done minimal study and reflection on worship (if any at all) and yet he was dictating policy to me. Worship had been my passionate focus in study, reflection, and practice for well over ten years. At his direction, I began to draw up a script for each worship service, a practice that I still do and have found to be quite helpful for those who lead and are in support roles. But the XP also expected me to recruit a team of people who would time each element of the service with a stopwatch and submit their findings to him. Being formed in part by the Charismatic influence of the Jesus People Movement, I thought that level of programming control seemed antithetical to Spirit-led worship.

The hardest challenge, however, came when the XP insisted that I take one of my core singers off of the praise team because of her weight. It was important to him that everyone on the platform convey a certain young and attractive look. Because she was somewhat overweight, she didn't qualify. It didn't matter that she had a consistent and dynamic Christian testimony and that she was one of my best singers. She didn't have the right look, so the XP did not want to have her on the platform. And, of course, I was supposed to be the one to tell her.

One of the senior leaders of the church later informed me that the XP had repeatedly tried to get me fired. Looking back, I know that I was wrong in some of my insubordination. But it was a clash of ministry philosophy. Some of the demands that were made of me conflicted with my deepest held values. In God's providence, church conflict from another arena caused the XP to resign and I stayed on. Such was my first encounter with the seeker-driven methodology inspired by Willow Creek Community Church.

A New Kind of Church

Evangelicalism in the late twentieth century witnessed the emergence of a new way of doing church that focused specifically on unbelievers who were spiritually curious. Churches that focused their mission on reaching these people were called "seeker-driven" or simply, "seeker churches." Of these churches, none has been more influential than Willow Creek Community Church in Chicago, Illinois. From the beginning, they were on the forefront of imagining new paradigms of evangelism within the context of a corporate gathering. Willow also received the greatest amount of attention from secular media, including features in *Time, Newsweek, Fortune,* and *Harvard Business Review* as well as several profiles produced for television specials.[2] Perhaps most importantly, Willow instituted its influence and methodology world-wide through the formation of the Willow Creek Association (WCA) in 1992 which, at its peak, included over 7,000 churches in over 90 denominations worldwide.[3]

Bill Hybels, co-founder and pastor of Willow Creek, could have hardly imagined what was to transpire when the church began in the fall of 1975. Hybels was groomed by his father to take over the lucrative family business in wholesale produce. But business classes in college bored him. And when he was

[2] Kimlon Howland Sargeant, *Seeker Churches: Promoting Traditional Religion in a Nontraditional Way,* (New Brunswick, New Jersey: Rutgers University Press, 2000) p. 9-10.

[3] WCA changed its focus primarily from local church support to leadership development through its annual *Global Leadership Summit* which is simulcast through hundreds of venues in North America and then translated into over fifty language to be presented around the world. While its reach has expanded exponentially through the Summit, church membership in the association, however, has declined significantly to about 2,000 churches in 2016.

challenged to do something with his life "that will last forever," it set him on a course of deep inner reflection. He left the family business and moved to Chicago to find his own path. In the summer of 1972, he connected with Dave Holmbo, with whom he had become friends through summer camps, and joined Holmbo's musical group, Son Company. Holmbo was the assistant music director at South Park Church and was an innovative and creative force. According to Holmbo, Hybels was just a "hack guitarist." But he was a gifted teacher. Shortly after Hybels joined Son Company, he started a Bible study after rehearsals for the group members and other interested young people.

It was the early 70s and spiritual revival was at its zenith in the Jesus People Movement. The Bible study quickly grew and by the spring of '73, Holmbo and Hybels launched a new ministry called "Son City" which dedicated a whole evening to reaching teenagers with the gospel. Through new and exciting music, engaging skits, and Bill's compelling and relevant teaching, the ministry exploded. Attendance and enthusiasm, however, were not the only significant developments. Students were responding to the gospel and the dynamic experience had a lasting effect on Hybels. Prompted by the overwhelming response of the students, the young pastor made a commitment that would shape his ministry into the future: "God, with your strength and for as long as I am in ministry I will always make sure that our strategy includes a regularly scheduled, high quality, Spirit-empowered outreach service where irreligious people can come and discover that they matter to You and that Christ died for them."[4]

By the summer of 1975, weekly attendance at Son City regularly surpassed 1,000. The early success that Hybels and Holmbo experienced in Son City would form the basis of a new kind of church ministry philosophy and methodology. At the same time, Hybels was coming under the compelling influence of Gilbert Bilezikian, Professor of Biblical Studies at nearby Trinity College. Bilezikian would challenge his students to embrace a

---

[4] Lynne and Bill Hybels, *Rediscovering Church: The Story and Vision of Willow Creek Community Church,* (Grand Rapids: Zondervan Publishing House, 1995), p. 40.

vision of a Spirit-empowered and transformational church that was irresistible. Bilezikian's words captured Hybels' imagination and passions. His ambition was expanding beyond youth ministry; he came to believe that "the church is the hope of the world." The stage was being set for a new venture that would reach not just young people, but adults as well. Hybels and Holmbo were all in and ready to plant a new kind of church.

Willow's Explosive Start

The new church launched its first service on Sunday morning, October 12, 1975 in the Willow Creek Theater in Palatine – a northern suburb of Chicago. One of the most remarkable facts about the new church was that each staff member was volunteer. No one received a salary at the beginning. Many would invest 30-40 hours a week in ministry and hold a part-time job to support themselves. And the work was hard. The production team typically would arrive at the theater at 4:00 AM for set-up and barely clear things out before the afternoon matinee began for the theater. As the ministry grew and families started attending, it became increasingly difficult to find adequate space for children's ministry. The members of the team that launched Willow in the early days were exceptionally talented, committed to the cause, and possessed a work ethic that wouldn't quit till the job was done right.

A year after Willow's launch, Hybels took the core team to Robert Schuller's pastor's conference in Garden Grove, California. He had been there the year before and was attracted to Schuller's innovative methods in reaching the unchurched people of Southern California. While at the conference, Hybels and his team had the opportunity to speak with Schuller privately in his office where the experienced innovator encouraged them to dream the impossible:

"If you give God a thimble, perhaps He will choose to fill it. If you give God a five-gallon bucket, perhaps He will choose to fill that. If you give Him a fifty-gallon drum, perhaps He will choose to do something extraordinary and fill even that. If

148

God chooses to do a miracle, you'd better be ready for it. Don't buy a thimbleful of land. Buy a fifty-gallon drum."[5]

A year later, in November, 1977, the young church purchased ninety acres of prime property in South Barrington for $660,000. Willow Creek Community Church was basking in the blessings of explosive growth and forward momentum.

The "Train Wreck"

But while Willow started with a bang, the new venture experienced a devastating recoil that threatened its viability. The ministry of Son City had been a true team effort. As the ministry expanded into a growing and dynamic church, however, the free-wheeling style of the staff began to impede its effectiveness as the demands of ministry increased. Willow's early leadership structure had no hierarchy of authority. While Hybels was tasked with coordinating the staff, he had no leverage to enforce his directives. And there was no accountability. In the spring of 1978, he called the team together, told them of the necessity of having one person serving at the point of leadership, and, in effect, nominated and appointed himself as the new Senior Pastor. At the young age of 26, Hybels also realized that he needed the covering and wisdom of an elder board which was established with four members later that year.

While some of the team welcomed the new structure of accountability, others resented the change and felt that Hybels was making a personal power play. Still, the Sunday morning ministry was growing, people were coming to Christ, and the staff had no time to work through their tensions. But the cohesive team that had started the church just three years earlier began to fracture. At the leadership's fall retreat that year, Hybels was confronted with the reality that a highly-valued team member was involved in patterns of behavior that threatened the integrity of the team and the well-being of the staff member's personal life. The crisis had to be dealt with. Because of the nature of the problem, however,

---

[5] *Ibid.*, p. 69.

Hybels and the elders decided to keep the matter private and insist on accountability and counseling for the staff member.

Along with staff tensions and a delicate personnel issue, the leadership team was also faced with the huge task of raising funds to build on their newly acquired prime property in Barrington. Armed with enough money and pledges, construction began for their new facility in June of 1979. But three months later, the train nearly went off the rails. The staff member involved in the destructive pattern of behavior had not responded to the course of direction given by the church elders. When they confronted him, he simply resigned. The elders' decision to keep the real reasons for his departure private led to turmoil and distrust among the staff. Within six months, nearly half of them would resign.

The tensions and challenges of 1978-1979 are known to Willow Creekers as "the Train Wreck." That the young leadership and church would not only survive but thrive is a testament to their determination, perseverance, and commitment to the vision that God had placed in their hearts. Of that season, Elder Laurie Pederson reflected:

> Before the Train Wreck, we were a bunch of young kids on a roll. Humility wasn't high on our list of character qualities. We thought we were pretty invincible. But the Train Wreck caused such incredible brokenness. As painful as it was, it served a God-honoring purpose. Real fruit can be born out of weakness.[6]

After the Train Wreck, Hybels' leadership and the ministry of Willow Creek began to mature. When Willow was first launched through the youth ministry of Son City, the leadership was primarily focused on the intense programming needs of the Sunday morning service and leading people to Christ. But over time and out of the painful lessons of the Train Wreck, they began to look deeply into the issues of accountability and transformational discipleship.

Recovery and Expansion

---

[6] *Ibid.,* p. 91.

On Sunday, February 15, 1981, Willow Creek Church finally moved into their new facility. The celebration that day was symbolic of the reality that the church had finally reached a new place of stability and was postured for even greater growth and influence. The national media began to take notice of the church, as several profiles of the ministry were done in both print and broadcast. For the next several years, Willow's reach would extend far beyond Chicago as Hybels began to share his model of seeker-driven churches at pastors' conferences. By the early nineties, a separate organization called the Willow Creek Association (WCA) was formed to meet the needs of the growing Seeker Church Movement. The formation of the WCA relieved the unbearable burden that Hybels and his staff had carried in leading both Willow Creek Community Church (which had grown to over 15,000 in weekly attendance) and spreading their influence around the world.

The scandal and allegations of Bill Hybel's abuse of power and sexual misconduct in 2018 was a shock to the evangelical world. Nevertheless, one of the strengths of Willow Creek and other seeker-driven churches has been their value of honest self-evaluation. In 2004, Willow commissioned Greg Hawkins and Callie Parkinson to do a self-study designed to discover the church's effectiveness in fostering real spiritual growth. The findings of the study can be found in a short book called, *Reveal: Where Are You?*[7] Hybels' response to *Reveal's* findings was characteristic to his focus on mission: "When I first heard these results, the pain of knowing was almost unbearable. Upon reflection, I realized that the pain of not knowing would be catastrophic."[8] Hybels set about refocusing some of Willow's priorities and reconfiguring their strategies to move believers into deeper spiritual maturity. Realizing, too, that their influence on other churches was very significant, Hawkins and Parkinson extended their survey findings and Willow's new strategies for

---

[7] Greg L. Hawkins, Cally Parkinson, and Eric Arnson, *Reveal: Where Are You,* Willow Creek Resources, 2007.
[8] *Ibid.,* p. 4.

spiritual growth in their book, *Move: What 1,000 Churches Reveal About Spiritual Growth.*[9]

Willow Creek Church and the seeker-driven model have made a very significant contribution to the evangelical landscape of the last nearly forty years. The WCA continues to promote their annual *Leadership Summit* around the world. The *Reveal* findings have impacted churches even outside of seeker-oriented ministries. But the ministry of Willow Creek Church and Bill Hybels is not without its detractors. Since the turn of the new century, mega-churches have come under increasing criticism from evangelical theologians, pastors, and writers – even as their numbers continue to grow. Books, papers, and blogs critical of the Seeker Movement are readily available.[10] In this chapter, however, I will seek to limit my critique primarily to the Seeker Movement's direct impact on corporate worship in evangelical churches.

Three Streams of Seeker-Movement Impact on Corporate Worship

The Seeker Movement is evangelical to its core. While some mainline churches have adopted the methodology, seeker churches have, nevertheless, been conservative rather than liberal in their theology and consider a personal "born-again experience" essential for salvation. As practical Evangelicals, seeker churches have been shaped by three primary influences: revivalism, business methodologies, and uniquely, "juvenilization." All three have a significant influence on corporate worship.

---

[9] Greg L. Hawkins and Cally Parkinson, *Move: What 1,000 Churches Reveal About Spiritual Growth,* Grand Rapids, Michigan: Zondervan, 2011.

[10] Perhaps the most thorough and fair of these critiques is G.A. Pritchard's *Willow Creek Seeker Services,* a reworking of the author's Ph.D. dissertation at Northwestern University in Chicago. Pritchard spent several years inside Willow Creek as an attender and had access to all the church's significant leaders. G.A. Pritchard, *Willow Creek Seeker Services: Evaluating a New Way of Doing Church* (Grand Rapids, MI: Baker Books, 1996).

Revivalism's Influence on the Seeker Movement

We have reviewed and critiqued revivalism's widespread influence on Evangelicals earlier in this book. Even a quick glance at the seeker-driven model of ministry reveals the revivalistic approach that Willow Creek used for its corporate gatherings. The purpose of Willow's seeker services was the same as Moody and Sankey's meetings a hundred years earlier: to move people to make a decision to receive Jesus Christ as their personal Savior.

Ever since Ira Sankey inspired people with his sensitive renditions of Victorian gospel songs, all revivalists have employed some kind of inspirational entertainment with varying degrees of intensity. Proponents of seeker services focused on engaging the audience's intellect and emotions through entertainment rather than inviting them into active involvement in corporate worship. They were very intentional in this regard. G.A. Prichard, however, notes a potential pitfall in this approach among seeker churches: "If a high priority is placed on providing entertainment rather than on communicating a message, the method will distort the message. The message will be distorted into a cheerful Christianity that is not true to the Scriptures."[11]

In the same way, with their heavy reliance upon the performing arts (music and drama), the seeker-driven model is highly susceptible to employing emotional manipulation to move individuals to a point of decision. Drama is especially effective in evoking emotions because of its ability to "reveal" thoughts, feelings, and concepts far beyond the dialogue in the script in what is called the "sub-text." And Willow excelled at producing effective Christian drama sketches that would move their audience. Prior to the emergence of Willow Creek's prominence, Christian drama was generally bad, being afflicted with an overreliance on sentimentality and the "easy answer." But Willow avoided such shallow pitfalls and instead relied almost exclusively on effective comedy or provocatively unmasking contemporary real problems that stirred uneasy questions that the speaker would then address in the message.

---

[11] *Ibid.*, p. 193.

Drama is a very powerful medium because of its unique ability to "reveal" truth. Done well, it almost always evokes a strong response from an audience or congregation. Drama can and should be used in both evangelism and worship. But it must be employed with the full awareness of its manipulative potential. Prichard observes that Willow Creek was quite aware of the power of the arts and intentionally avoided the temptation to manipulate their audience. Unfortunately, as the seeker model passed from Willow on to thousands of other churches, the wisdom and insight that came with the original innovation did not always follow, and too often in other settings, the means unintentionally trumped the gospel message.

One of the enduring legacies of the Seeker Movement was the insistence on preaching to the "felt needs" of the people. It was a savvy approach that built large and successful ministries. I attended several conferences and staff meetings where the topic under consideration was how we could market and strategize our ministry programs to hit the felt

> *One of the enduring legacies of the Seeker Movement was the insistence on preaching to the "felt needs" of the people.*

needs of people. Disney was often held up as the model for ministry programming exemplified in their films (the successful formula of "laughter and tears") and the hospitality of their theme parks.

To be sure, there is wisdom to be found for ministry in some of the practices of secular companies. "Common grace" informs us that the church does not have a lock on everything there is to know about relating with other people. But the premise of beginning with the felt-needs of people is a faulty foundation upon which to build corporate worship and other ministries for the church. Such an approach is human-centered rather than God-centered. Basing our ministry on the felt-needs of people is accommodation to the culture. It eventually leads the church astray into a consumeristic approach to Christianity. Consumerism in worship and the church has led us to these unfortunate conditions in the modern American church:

"Worship wars:" In many churches, the so-called "worship wars" have pretty much abated as the Builder Generation has died off and band-led music has generally become the dominant genre in evangelical worship. But the consumerist impulse to have individual preferences satisfied in the music that we sing has created high levels of tensions in congregations for nearly a whole generation. Moreover, in the effort to meet the musical preferences of worshippers, many churches adopted a multiple service - multiple style approach that, in effect, formed different churches.[12]

"Church hopping:" "If the church doesn't provide the kind of music or worship that I like, I can just go down the street. If the preacher doesn't measure up to the podcast that I listen to, well, I might just as well stay home and listen to him."

Shallow criticism: If the first impulse of the church is to meet the "felt-needs" of the people, then the congregation will be trained to expect personal satisfaction. Evaluation of the worship experience, then, becomes based on false criteria such as whether or not it was upbeat and emotionally moving. If it isn't, worship leaders can expect to hear from the people and, perhaps more threateningly, from the XP. The important values of biblical, trinitarian, and Christ-focus are lost when

---

[12] Multiple worship services based on style preference do, indeed, form another congregation with different DNA because music tends to form the culture and soul of a people. In my own experience, a church I served chose to have different services to quell the discontent of two factions. The leadership would not accept that it formed two different congregations, but their assertions proved otherwise when the church could not pass (by vote) significant ministry initiatives. Contemporary service attenders tended to be progressive in their approach to ministry, while traditionalists were resistant to many changes. Instead of doing the hard work of helping the people to live with each other's differences, the two factions remained stuck in their inflexibility towards each other. They were, indeed, two different churches.

the first premise of worship planning is meeting the felt-needs of people.

Religious consumers: The true nature of Christian faith is humility and submission to Christ and others. When the foundation upon which we build our corporate worship gatherings is to meet the "felt-needs" of people, we are forming them into religious consumers focused on themselves. Such a concept is opposite to the New Testament's idea of a Jesus-follower.

Biblical illiteracy: The alarming lack of biblical knowledge in American congregations is attributable to many factors. But the rise of topical "felt-needs" messages as opposed to systematic exegetical preaching has certainly contributed to the inability of many modern Christians to study the Bible for themselves.

Fortunately, many church leaders are beginning to wake up and be alarmed by rampant consumerism in the American church. Books and blogs against religious consumerism abound. But rooting it out will take courage and focused determination on the part of emerging leaders. Religious consumerism, unfortunately, is a stubborn legacy of the Seeker-Driven Movement.

Like other revivalistic approaches to corporate worship, Willow Creek and the Seeker Movement placed their primary focus on bringing "Unchurched Harry and Mary"[13] to a point of decision for Christ. Early on, Hybels did recognize the need for spiritual formation in small groups and in a midweek service designed especially for believers. But neither small groups nor the midweek service received near the attention and resources that the Sunday seeker services received. The shortcoming of the seeker focus in forming "fully devoted followers of Jesus Christ" was exposed in the *Reveal* study of 2004. Of course, seeker churches are not alone in their ineffectiveness in forming Christian disciples. Every evangelical church knows it must be evangelistic.

---

[13] Willow Creek's label for their "target audience" of unbelievers.

It is in our DNA. But evangelism as we usually understand it – bringing people to a point conversion – must also be balanced with discipleship. One of the churches that I served as Senior Pastor had been an evangelistic church with its own TV broadcast for over fifty years. The focus was to bring people to make a decision for Christ and not much more beyond that. The unfortunate by-product was an unusually large number of adult "prodigals" who had left the faith and people in the congregation who were willing, but did not know how to grow spiritually. Seeker-driven churches who do not give the same attention and resources to discipleship will reap the same disappointing results.

Finally, Willow Creek's influence on the structure of worship for other evangelical churches would be hard to overstate. With the explosion in popularity of seeker services in the 90s and the establishment of the WCA to "franchise" the methodology, the consumerist/revivalist approach to corporate worship has shaped the understanding of many evangelical churches and produced its unintended

...consumerist/revivalist approach to corporate worship has shaped the understanding of many evangelical churches and produced its unintended fruit well into the twenty-first century.

fruit well into the twenty-first century. Moreover, while Willow attempted to provide a pathway to discipleship through midweek services, not all churches that followed the seeker-driven model for the weekend balanced their evangelistic emphasis with discipleship intention and resources. There were many congregations that adapted seeker methodology for weekend services that were intended to reach both believers and "Unchurched Harry" with a "seeker-sensitive" approach. Unfortunately, the same negative worship outcomes that plagued seeker-driven churches would also afflict, to some degree, seeker-sensitive services.

Church as a Business

Bill Hybels inherited his father's business acumen and applied it to his approach to church ministry. Its effectiveness, in terms of numerical growth, is unarguable. As seeker methodology for corporate gatherings began to spread in the 80s and 90s, so too did Willow's business approach to church ministry. In my own experience, I have read and processed business leadership books together with the rest of church staff since the late 80s. Church leaders still promote and use methodology from the business world in church ministry. I don't know how many times I've read or heard Jim Collins' metaphor of "getting the right people on the bus, sitting in the right seat, and the wrong people off the bus."[14] It's a helpful metaphor. I've used it myself.

Using business methodology can be helpful in the same "common grace" way that the church can adopt some performance and hospitality values from Disney. The problem is not "borrowing" from the wisdom of secular sources, *per se,* but rather borrowing *uncritically,* without considering possible outcomes that conflict with biblical values and practice. Unfortunately, with the practical evangelical impulse to reach the most people, we've often rushed to adapt methodologies that might increase outward effectiveness while unintentionally reaping inward rottenness in our corporate soul.

The effect of business methodology on what should be a transcendent divine engagement in worship is especially troubling. For seeker-driven and sensitive churches, weekend gatherings became programs rather than worship services. The changing nomenclature was telling of the significant paradigm shift that was occurring. The "sanctuary" became the "auditorium" and the "platform" became the "stage." The "pulpit" was now called a "lectern" or "podium." Indeed, the art of designing and leading

---

[14] Collins introduced the metaphor in his book, *From Good to Great* (New York, New York, Harper Collins, 2001) and you can also find it in a blog post on his website: http://www.jimcollins.com/article_topics/articles/good-to-great.html (Accessed 12/31/2016).

the elements of the gathering was called "programming" in seeker terminology.[15]

The direct effect on corporate worship was to turn what was to be a God-focused meeting into a program driven by market and consumer preference. "Programming" staff evaluated the gatherings based primarily on performance criteria rather than transformative value. Pastors and ministry staff, sadly, became "success-driven" in order to attract more and more people and keep up with the mega-church on the other side of town. The business model and the drive for the highest quality necessary to attract and keep religious consumers becomes a vicious cycle of greed and futility. Quality and innovation are not cheap. Costs keep rising and it becomes necessary to put more people in the seats and add more and more to the giving rolls. Competition among large evangelical churches is fierce. And the vast majority of churches that are relatively small can't (mercifully) play in the game.

But the most damning effect of the employment of business methodology in corporate worship is that it eliminates any supernatural sense of engaging with God.[16] The service is heavily scripted down to the minute. Pastor A.W. Tozer called such folly "substituting the program for the Presence." His critique, published in 1955, is sobering and prescient for today:

> The point we make here is that in our times the program has been substituted for the Presence. The program rather than the Lord of glory is the center of attraction. So the most popular gospel church in any city is likely to be the one that offers the most interesting program; that is, the church that can present the most and best feature for the enjoyment of the

---

[15] For many years, the WCA maintained an online job board where those seeking positions in music and worship leadership in churches accessed listings on the "programming" page.

[16] See John Jefferson Davis, *Worship and the Reality of God: An Evangelical Theology of Real Presence* (Downers Grove: Intervarsity Press, 2010) for an in-depth theological analysis, critique, and corrective for the loss of divine presence in evangelical corporate worship.

public. These features are programed so as to keep everything moving and everyone expectant.

The evil of it all lies in its effect upon Christians and churches everywhere. Even persons who may honestly desire to serve God...are deceived by the substitution of the program for the Presence, with the result that they never really become mature Christians. Their appetites are debauched and their sense of spiritual values dwarfed at the very beginning of their religious lives. Many of them go on year after year totally unaware that the program they go to see and hear each Sunday is not a Christian thing at all but a pagan concept superimposed upon the church by zealous but misled persons.[17]

Juvenilization

In my opinion, Willow Creek has been and continues to be "youth ministry on steroids." Willow Creek Community Church emerged from the ministry of Son City. The same methodology that Hybels and Holmbo used to attract teenagers in the seventies was, and still is, employed by the church. The characteristics of youth ministry that targeted Boomers are pervasive in the seeker-driven model:

- The exclusive use of popular music styles
- Youthful look and approach
- The aversion to anything traditional like choirs and hymns
- The elimination of most sacred symbols
- The primacy of "relevance"
-

Tom Bergler, Professor of Ministry at Huntington University published the central thesis of his doctoral dissertation in his book, *The Juvenilization of American Christianity*.[18] In the book,

---

[17] A.W. Tozer, *The Root of the Righteous*, (Harrisburg, PA: Christian Publications, Inc. 1955), p. 95.

[18] Thomas E. Bergler, *The Juvenilization of American Christianity*, (Grand Rapids: The William B. Eerdmans Publishing Company, 2012).

Bergler documents the developments of youth ministries after World War II which mirrored America's obsession with youth culture during the same period. Prior to the war, professional youth ministers in the church, as we know them today, did not exist. But after the trauma of World War II and potential horror of nuclear annihilation, Americans wanted to preserve and focus on their future. Youth culture was celebrated through popular icons such as James Dean, Marlon Brando, and Elvis Presley. Television programming celebrated youth culture even more with American Bandstand, Soul Train, and the Ed Sullivan Show, to name just a few popular platforms. The first American president of the sixties was youthful and his focus was on the "New Frontier." Progressive cultures based on the Enlightenment principles of modernism are bound to focus on the future. Americans since the end of World War II have been obsessed with youth.

Evangelicals, in particular, shifted a lot of their focus and resources towards youth ministry at the same time. Bergler documents the significant growth of the para-church youth ministries Young Life and Youth for Christ (YFC) during the post-war years. Unrestricted by the constraints of church boards and tradition-oriented constituencies, para-church youth ministries were very creative in employing means to attract and evangelize young people. Leaders would hold Saturday night rallies that would feature new Christian music in popular musical styles. Ralph Carmichael, who would go on to become one of the most important innovators in Contemporary Christian Music, employed big band stylings in the music he led at YFC rallies in Los Angeles.[19]

When they could, YFC and Young Life would also recruit Christian celebrities to appear at the rallies to imply that it's "cool to be a Christian." The use of Christian celebrity testimonials was also effectively used by Billy Graham in his crusades and it was the stock and trade of Robert Schuller in his "Hour of Power" broadcasts. While Willow never relied as heavily on celebrity

---

[19] Thomas E. Bergler in *Wonderful Words of Life: Hymns in American Protestant History and Theology,* Richard J. Mouw and Mark A. Noll, eds. (Grand Rapids: William B. Eerdmans, 2004) p. 125.

appearances in their seeker services as Schuller did, they would make an occasional appearance. The important point, however, is that para-church youth ministries strove to present an image of Christianity that was up-to-date, cool, and relevant.

When Dave Holmbo and Bill Hybels were doing youth ministry in Son City, they held the same values and employed the same programming methodology as the para-church groups did in their Saturday night rallies. Bergler observes:

> Youth leaders had succeeded in creating a juvenilized version of Christianity that marketed the old-time religion in the trappings of the youth counterculture. And in subsequent decades, seeker-service pioneers like Bill Hybels and Rick Warren would use the same techniques to attract Baby Boomer adults to church.[20]

An essential component to the ministry strategy of Young Life and YFC was to target student athletes and cheerleaders who were attractive and popular. The rationale was straightforward: teenagers want to be cool and if the popular kids are involved in the youth ministry, the others will follow. Willow Creek, by design or by intuition, seemed to adopt the same strategy for those who would appear on their stage. Prichard observed:

> "All participants in the service are highly skilled and thoroughly prepared. They also are generally attractive people who are well-dressed. Unchurched visitors 'see excellence,' as evangelism director [Mark] Mittleberg explains, 'sharp people out there singing and in dramas.'"[21]

The strategy of exclusively using good-looking, talented people on the platform begs an important question, however. Where can a church member who is not of semi-professional musical caliber or perhaps not so physically attractive use their gifts in ministry? As the story at the beginning of this chapter shows, the use of the

---

[20] Bergler, *The Juvenilization of American Christianity*, p. 205.
[21] Prichard, p. 102.

"youthful-attractive" rubric can be very damaging to people and deprive the church of significant gifts of service. While always having very talented and good-looking people on the platform may have appealed to "unchurched Harry and Mary," it seems to me that such an exclusive approach is elitist and contrary to what Jesus taught in the Beatitudes. He never said, "Blessed are the good-looking and talented – the 'winners in life's lottery.'" Rather, he affirmed the poor-in-spirit and the meek.

Bill Hybels is a Baby Boomer. Boomers were all about overthrowing "the Establishment" – the status quo. True to Boomer values, Willow Creek eschewed most anything that was traditional. In seeker churches, you likely won't find organs, traditional choirs, robes, or hymnals. Bulletins are "worship folders" or announcement sheets. Printed orders of worship are replaced by timed worship scripts seen only by platform personnel and production teams. Pulpits and Communion Tables are replaced by a business-like lectern. Sometimes, even crosses are hard to find.

Nothing traditional is allowed. That's a pretty rigid box. Church leaders who subscribe to the seeker paradigm generally consider themselves innovators and free-thinkers. But I have found some seeker church leaders to be even more rigid in their thinking than many who don't approve of the methodology. Jim (not his real name) was an adult ministries pastor and a

> *[Jesus] never said, "Blessed are the good-looking and talented-the 'winners in life's lottery.'"*

proponent of seeker methodology as well as a colleague of mine for a couple of years. When he was applying for his position as Adult Pastor, I enthusiastically promoted hiring him because I thought his energy and innovative perspective would benefit our conservative church. His perspective did indeed "refresh" many of our ministries but we often chaffed when it came to ideas about corporate worship because he wanted to eliminate every traditional element that we had. No hymns or hymnals and eliminate the choir. The formula was familiar. What seemed ironic to me was that while I was open and had adopted many of his ideas, Jim was adamant that all tradition should be eliminated from corporate worship. To be bound by a paradigm that demands constant innovation to the exclusion of meaningful tradition is neither a virtue nor freedom. Enslavement to novelty is a prison equal to rigid traditional churches that prohibit guitars and drums.

In a similar sense, the exclusive use of contemporary worship bands has also impoverished the church from using a whole generation of traditional wind and string players who have very few opportunities to use and cultivate their gifts to glorify God in corporate worship.[22] It is true that there is some music available for string and wind players in the contemporary praise and worship genre.[23] But few churches utilize these resources. They are relatively expensive, and traditional instruments with contemporary songs are not always a good musical fit.[24] Traditional hymns, on the other hand, lend themselves very well to the use of wind and string instruments.[25]

The same problem exists for the exclusion of singers who are not soloist quality (and good-looking). The role of a praise team vocalist demands that the singer be of soloist caliber and able to harmonize. Not everyone who enjoys singing can be on the praise team. Certain advanced skills are required. In traditional churches, singers who could not harmonize "by ear" and sing

---

[22] As Willow's music ministry matured, traditional instruments and orchestra were added from time to time. Willow, however, had the resources to employ staff arrangers and had a deep pool of talented musicians to pull off the quality they expected. Most churches that followed Willow's model do not have the same luxuries.

[23] Word Music has published a series of orchestrations for traditional instruments called *Songs of Praise and Worship* in several volumes. *Praisecharts.com* provides orchestrations for contemporary worship songs.

[24] Praise and worship music, by nature, needs a measure of flexibility (as in spontaneous repeats) but traditional instrumentalists are generally dependent upon reading the music on the page. I have found that most do not have that kind of flexibility unless they have some jazz experience.

[25] Word Music and Lillenas publish excellent idiomatic orchestrations to accompany their hymns.

solos could enjoy singing in the choir. Seeker churches, of course, banned traditional choirs. Some have effectively utilized "praise choirs" to accompany the praise team and provide an avenue of service for these singers. But praise choirs don't demand the same choral discipline or skill as a good traditional choir, so the level of satisfaction for experienced singers will be significantly diminished. Still, these casual choirs can be effective and they do provide an outlet for musical expression. It may be impractical to expect churches that are exclusively band-driven to employ choirs and traditional hymns with orchestrations, but nevertheless, the lack of opportunity for these musicians is an overlooked but significant loss for the congregation.

Finally, ministries that are "juvenilized" pursue cultural relevance as a singular focused quest. The two go hand-in-hand. Relevance isn't the problem. If we define relevance as "the quality of relating to a matter in hand with pertinence and appropriateness," then the followers of Jesus should be, of all people, the most relevant.[26] Christ is the same, yesterday, today, and forever. Relevance is essential to the Mission of God. But *seeking relevance for its own sake and without careful reflection* is a cultural trap that can endanger the essence of the gospel, a trap that Evangelicals have been all too prone to step into. Bergler shows that the danger of fully accommodating our ministry to a youth-obsessed culture is that our growth and maturity in Christ will be stunted. This is a very serious concern for the American church in the twenty-first century. He warns:

> ...Evangelicals led the way in developing a version of adolescent Christianity that would come to dominate both youth ministries and the churches in the decades ahead. Unfortunately, their success came at some cost. By assuming that teen tastes in music and spirituality were essentially neutral, they allowed youth culture the power to reshape Christian faith. While some of these changes were beneficial, others would create a chronic immaturity among American Christians. The

---

[26] Os Guinness, *Prophetic Untimeliness: A Challenge to the Idol of Relevance* (Grand Rapids: Baker Books, 2003) p. 12.

sixties revealed once and for all that adolescent Christianity would shape the future of the churches one way or the other. It could not be ignored.[27]

Corrective Initiatives

I once had the opportunity to dine with several leaders in music and higher education which included a very well-known gospel lyricist. Our conversation eventually moved to developments in contemporary worship. When I raised the topic of seeker-driven methodology, the lyricist suggested that the movement had no redeeming qualities whatsoever and that it had wreaked tremendous damage on the worship life of the church. I was a bit taken back by her complete rejection of seeker methodology but understood the passionate reaction. The seeker approach to doing corporate worship has come at a significant cost to the spiritual health and vitality of the church. Even Bill Hybels admits as much from the findings of the *Reveal* study.

As was shown in the chapter on Revivalism, correction and renewal begins with reflection on the nature and mission of the church. Bringing people to a point of decision and conversion is central to the identity and mission of seeker-oriented churches. But, as we have seen, the initial conversion experience is only the beginning of a Christian's journey. Discipleship and spiritual formation must follow. We

> *The seeker approach to doing corporate worship has come at a significant cost to the spiritual health and vitality of the church.*

need to be "brought into" Christ as much as we need to be "led to" Christ. The lesson from Revivalism's short-sided legacy also reminds us that corporate worship is an essential ingredient in Christian formation. As a direct offspring of Revivalism, seeker methodology also undervalued corporate worship for spiritual

---

[27] Bergler, p. 207.

formation. Even further, seeker proponents failed to recognize that the methods they used in attracting seekers to their church also negatively formed them into self-focused religious consumers. Pastors and staff became religious-business innovators and sales personnel who ran the never-ending treadmill of filling seats and coffers. Indeed, even their jobs and salary were tied to increasing metrics in the vicious cycle. John Jefferson Davis suggests in *Worship and the Reality of God:*

> ...making the unchurched the primary focus of Sunday morning is a flawed and unbiblical strategy. This element of the evangelical and revival tradition, reaching from Charles Finney to Bill Hybels, which displaced the centrality of worship in the life of the church with evangelism, may now have passed its peak and deserves to be laid to rest.[28]

Much has been and is being written to confront and correct the shortcomings of the seeker-driven church. The point to be made here is that corporate worship is central to the mission of the church – that of "making disciples."[29] Seeker churches focused on the attractional value of corporate gatherings. And while seeker methodology, in its purest sense, did not consider weekend services to be corporate worship (that's what was done in mid-week believer services), over time, the paradigms of seeker programing were adopted by seeker-sensitive churches in their Sunday corporate worship. In a sense, worship elements, including songs which were intended to facilitate the engagement of people with God, were "prostituted" simply for attractional purposes. That was the message I heard from consultants in the 1980s who insisted that churches embrace the new worship music and jettison the old in order to bring the Boomers back to church.

There is perhaps no more pressing issue regarding seeker methodology and worship than juvenilization. Praise and worship

---

[28] Davis, p. 29.

[29] See James K. A. Smith's book, *You Are What You Love: The Spiritual Power of Habit,* especially chapters 3 and 4 for compelling reasons to re-conceptualize and re-structure corporate worship for effective discipleship. (Grand Rapids: Brazos Press, 2016)

music, by its very dynamic nature, will always be driven by youthful values. It will always be seeking the "new sound" that is popular. It is, after all, "pop(ular)" music. Its strength is its relevance. Its potential shortcoming is its shallowness. In his book, Bergler devotes a significant amount of time criticizing the romantic nature of many contemporary praise and worship songs. Since romance is a significant issue for young people, it is not surprising that yearning for life-long companionship would also appear as an echoed theme in spiritual yearning. Romantic imagery and examples abound. Here are just a few:

"Jesus, I am so in love with you..." *Let My Words Be Few* by Matt Redman

"Nothing compares to your embrace..." *Forever Reign* by Jason Ingram and Rueben Morgan

"There's no place I'd rather be than in your arms of love..." *Arms of Love* by Craig Musseau

There is, as the chapter on Pietism has shown, a long mystical tradition merging erotic yearning with spirituality. The significant difference, as noted in the discussion of Pietism, is that classic Christian mystical yearning involved self-abnegation whereas modern romantic yearning is for self-fulfillment. Bergler wonders and warns:

...is the music we sing in church fostering a self-centered, romantic spirituality in which following Jesus is compared to "falling in love?" If so, we should not be surprised if some people have a relationship with Jesus that has all the maturity and staying power of an adolescent infatuation.[30]

It is incumbent upon pastors, worship leaders, and lay leaders to ensure the texts that their church sings in corporate worship are moving the people into spiritual maturity. Leaders must

---

[30] Bergler, p. 227.

recognize the juvenilization effect in the broader American culture and carefully discern the musical diet that is being fed to their congregation.

In this book, we have rehearsed the stories of Pietism and Revivalism. Seeker churches have inherited the negative impact on corporate worship discussed in both chapters. Additionally, the Seeker-Church Movement has amplified the shortcomings of Pietism and Revivalism even more to remain "relevant" to an increasingly autonomous and juvenilized culture. Worship renewal initiatives discussed previously are pertinent to churches that wish to move away from seeker methodology. Fortunately, many Millennials are reconsidering tradition in their faith formation. Many in the "Emerging Church" phenomenon of the early 2000's embraced church tradition in their corporate worship. Perhaps as a reaction against the Boomer values of their parents, many Millennials prefer tradition over contemporary worship genres.[31] When I visited *City Light Church* in the hip, revitalized neighborhood of Benson, Omaha, I was surprised that all their worship songs were hymns rearranged for band. Tradition is making a comeback with younger Evangelicals. Boomer church leaders sometimes wrongly assume that all of the corporate worship music has to be band-driven contemporary worship songs in order to attract younger people.

But moving away from the seeker-attractional model comes at a cost for churches seeking deeper discipleship and renewal. Pastor Walt Kallestad embraced emerging seeker paradigms in the 1980s and led his 200-member Lutheran church into explosive growth. The Community Church of Joy in Phoenix would eventually grow to draw over 12,000 people with professional musicians, a huge facility, and a successful school. But a medical crisis in 2002 caused Kallestad to take a sabbatical for rest and reflection. During that time, he realized that he was spinning his wheels into self-destruction and that the ministry of the church was ineffective in developing mature disciples of Jesus. His self-

---

[31] Anecdotally, I've encountered many who prefer hymns over contemporary praise and worship and know of many who have left their low-church worship congregations and united with traditional liturgical churches such as Lutheran, Anglican, and Orthodox.

reflection led him to similar conclusions that *Reveal* had brought to Bill Hybels. The Community Church of Joy was producing "consumers – like Pac-Man, gobbling up religious experiences, navigating a maze but going nowhere in particular."[32]

While on sabbatical, Kallestad visited emergent, missional, and Charismatic churches where he encountered the power of God in their gatherings. People were healed and worshippers engaged wholeheartedly. It wasn't a show or a performance. It wasn't scripted and professional. There was passion and fire. God showed up!

When Kallestad returned from his leave, he began overhauling the whole paradigm of ministry at the Community Church of Joy. The professional musicians who had brought the best music money could buy were dismissed and replaced with those who would genuinely lead the congregation into engagement with God in worship. Of course, the musical quality waned and the crowds began to diminish as the religious consumers began to be dissatisfied. Overall, Kallestad lost over a third of his congregation. But the pruning also brought a new sense of mission and greater spiritual fruit as people actually began to grow in their faith. The church would continue to grow in its expectation of encountering God in worship to the point that it would embrace a Charismatic identity and merge with Dream City Church in 2016.

Kent Carlson and Mike Lueken tell a similar story about the transformation of Oak Hills Church in Folsom, California in their book, *Renovation of the Church*.[33] Their "epiphany" came at a staff retreat as they were digesting church-growth "guru" Lyle Shaller's book, *The Very Large Church*.[34] In the book, they were confronted with the realities of the religious consumer culture they were feeding at Oak Hills. Together, the staff "began to realize that, to be faithful to the gospel of Jesus, consumerism was not a force to

---

[32] Kallestad and Wilson, *"Showtime!" No More.*

[33] Kent Carlson and Mike Lueken, *Renovation of the Church: What Happens When a Seeker Church Discovers Spiritual Formation,* (Downers Grove, IL: Intervarsity Press, 2011).

[34] Lyle E. Schaller, *The Very Large Church: New Rules for Leaders,* (Nashville, TN: Abingdon Press, 2000).

be harnessed but rather an antibiblical value system that had to be prophetically challenged."[35]

Unlike the Community Church of Joy, Oak Hills made the transition away from the seeker model gradually. The challenge of losing a good portion of the congregation, however, was the same. It was painful to downsize the staff. But the result of their "renovation" was a complete rethinking of holistic church ministry, including structure, spiritual formation, outreach, and worship. While the Community Church of Joy took the path of Charismatic renewal in their worship, Oak Hills followed many of the teachings of worship renewalist Robert E. Webber in his "ancient-future" paradigms.

Summary and Path to Renewal

Willow Creek Community Church was birthed in the exciting days of the Jesus People Movement as a youth ministry. The ensuing Seeker Church Movement emerged in the eighties as the impulse of the Jesus People Movement became institutionalized. Following in the wake of the Jesus People Movement, the Seeker Movement seems fresh in our historical portrait album. The portraits of Willow and the Seeker Movement are contemporary and vivid. While Hybels is no longer leading Willow Creek Community Church, its influence remains widely felt. Still, enough time has passed since its beginning that historical and practical reflection on the Seeker Movement is helpful for church and worship leaders.

Willow's story is inspiring through the hard work of its leaders and the ways in which God moved to establish the congregation. It is a vivid and exciting portrait in our evangelical narrative. Willow's explosive growth led the methodology to become a model which thousands of other evangelical churches would emulate through the 1980s and 90s. Seeker churches were effective in co-opting the cultural milieu of consumerism and juvenilization into their ministry strategy to grow exceptionally

---

[35] Carlson and Lueken, p. 35.

large churches. But the price of "success" was diminished discipleship and the formation of "religious consumers."

While there has always been pushback against seeker methodology, it has increased since the turning of the century. Younger generations are not so keen to adopt Boomer methodology and many leaders are rightly recognizing the spiritual costs of religious consumerism. Churches that choose to move away from seeker methodology generally do so because they have discovered that they are deficient in producing transforming disciples of Jesus. While the pathway towards renewal comes with a significant cost, many leaders have opted for renewal in order to become faithful to the counter-cultural mission of the gospel.

In his insightful book, *Prophetic Untimeliness,* Os Guiness calls the church to practice "faithful relevance" which holds the evangelical imperative of relevance and the wisdom of tradition in tension:

> By our uncritical pursuit of relevance we have actually courted irrelevance; by our breathless chase after relevance without a matching commitment to faithfulness, we have become not only unfaithful but irrelevant; by our determined efforts to redefine ourselves in ways that are more compelling to the modern world than are faithful to Christ, we have lost not only our identity but our authority and our relevance. Our crying need is to be *faithful* as well as *relevant*.[36] [Emphasis mine.]

I believe that worship renewal for Evangelicals that is both faithful and relevant will have the following characteristics:

Our worship communicates the gospel without confusion. The gospel is not distorted or diluted by accommodation to culture. The gospel transcends culture. Pastors and worship leaders should be always diligent to make the substance of the corporate worship that they plan and lead Christo-centric. Be sure that all song texts are biblically sound and aligned with the gospel. Be especially aware of the

---

[36] Guiness, p. 15.

tendency of contemporary songs to conform with juvenilized or consumer-oriented cultural values.

Our worship is local rather than franchised. Seeker churches franchised their way of doing ministry based on successful business models. But real relevance can't be franchised. Relevance is always local because localities are always unique. Engage critical thinking before adopting ministry methodologies and ask whether or not it fits your congregation and community.

Our worship balances tradition with innovation. Tradition is the best corrective to our culture's never-ending quest for the new. Traditional forms such as creeds, prayers, and hymns can be given up-to-date settings without diluting their essence. The Emerging Church of the early 2000's effectively worked many of the Church's ancient forms into their corporate worship. The move of some Boomers and many younger Evangelicals toward more liturgical traditions such as Anglican, Catholic, and Orthodox should encourage worship planners and leaders to "innovate with tradition."

Our worship seeks to find its place in the Greater Story. One of modernism's biggest flaws is its tendency to jettison the past, glorify the present, and overstate the future. In so doing modernism has no story, but is stuck in a self-centered whirlpool that has no destination. The Christian Story, on the other hand, has a history, a present, and certain future. This is where inclusion of traditional elements will be very helpful. Tradition empowers the church to impart its congregation with an identity. Church traditions (creeds, hymns, liturgy) serve as a sort of "picture album" or narrative of our spiritual ancestors.

The seeker methodology of Willow Creek Community Church was very effective in swelling the numbers of thousands of evangelical churches. It was equally effective in afflicting the church with a generation of religious consumers. Renewal is critical if the church is to recover its counter-cultural mission of transformation. "Faithful relevance," applied to our corporate worship practice, is a good starting place.

173

Questions for Reflection:

1. Do you find any ideas or qualities from the Seeker-Church Movement to be biblically faithful and helpful in your own church? Give examples and support your answer.

2. Has seeker methodology negatively impacted the corporate worship of your church? Give examples and explain the specific negative impact to the mission of the church.

3. Are your church leaders afraid of tradition? If so, what do you suppose is behind their fears? How could you "innovate with tradition" in your setting?

4. Do you observe manifestations of juvenilization in your own congregation? What specific ways would you address the mindset and its negative impact?

5. What specific ways do you address religious consumerism in your church?

Suggested Reading:

Bergler, Thomas E., *The Juvenilization of American Christianity*, (Grand Rapids: William B. Eerdman's Publishing Company, 2012).

_____, *From Here to Maturity: Overcoming the Juvenilization of American Christianity*, (Grand Rapids: William B. Eerdman's Publishing Company, 2014).

Carlson, Kent and Lueken, Mike, *Renovation of the Church: What Happens When a SeekerChurch Discovers Spiritual Formation*, (Downers Grove, IL: Intervarsity Press, 2011).

Davis, John Jefferson, *Worship and the Reality of God: An Evangelical Theology of Real Presence*, (Downers Grove, IL: Intervarsity Press, 2010).

Dawn, Marva J., *A Royal "Waste" of Time: The Splendor of Worshiping God and Being Church for the World*, (Grand Rapids: William B. Eerdmans Publishing Company, 1999).

Guiness, Os, *Prophetic Untimeliness: A Challenge to the Idol of Relevance,* (Grand Rapids: Baker Books, 2003).

Kennedy, Rodney Wallace and Hatch, Derek C., *Gathering Together: Baptists at Work in Worship,* (Eugene, OR: Wipf and Stock Publishers, 2013).

MacDonald, G. Jeffrey, *Thieves in the Temple: The Christian Church and the Selling of the American Soul,* (New York: Perseus Books Group, 2010).

Pritchard, G.A., *Willow Creek Seeker Services: Evaluating a New Way of Doing Church,* (Grand Rapids: Baker Books, 1996).

Smith, James K. A., *You Are What You Love: The Spiritual Power of Habit,* (Grand Rapids: Brazos Pres, 2016).

How Shall We Then Worship?

"...in many ways I think the future of orthodox, faithful, robust Christianity hinges on the renewal of worship."

James K.A. Smith
You Are What You Love

The 1960s and 70s were turbulent years for the United States. Though the nation triumphed in its quest to reach the moon and made significant progress in long-overdue civil rights reforms, the stable and halcyon days of the previous decade were shaken by the sexual revolution, anti-establishment rock culture, rampant drug abuse, riots, the Vietnam War, and the resignation of a disgraced president. The assassination of three beloved national leaders within the decade was symbolic of the upheaval American culture endured during the 60's.

Evangelicals, of course, were not untouched by the turbulence. Many began to trace and analyze world events in anticipation of Christ's immanent Second Coming. The biggest reaction to the upheaval, of course, was the Jesus People Movement, discussed in Chapter 5. Evangelicals also began to mobilize politically, notably aligning with conservatives through the "Moral Majority" to oppose abortion, which was legalized in 1973, and to try and address what was perceived as an increasing slide into moral depravity. In 1976, Francis A. Schaffer, the most popular evangelical philosopher of the day, published a book and produced a film series intending to address the causes and effects of the decline of Western Culture. *How Shall We Then Live?* traced Western thought and practice from the Roman Empire through

The Middle Ages, The Reformation, and 20th Century Modernism.[1] Schaffer's survey of historical movements and people was intended to inform his contemporary readers how their culture had evolved and devolved to arrive at its declining state. He also posited some possible correctives from a biblical and Christian perspective.

What Schaffer intended to do on a broad cultural scale, I have tried to do focusing on evangelical worship practices. We have traced historical people and moments that have shaped and influenced the way that we worship with the intent that we may have greater understanding of why we do what we do. The portraits that we have uncovered in our family picture album have fulfilled the four benefits of historical study and reflection noted in the introduction. From Luther and Zwingli to the Seeker Church, we have gained insight on evangelical DNA and why we worship as we do today. A common theme throughout each of the stories we have considered is the focus, ingenuity, and perseverance of the people who served God's purpose in their generation. Their dedication to their calling is truly inspirational and a model for Evangelicals today. From the perspective of historical distance, we have also dissected the unintended consequences of the movements that we have considered. People spend hours in a therapist's office trying to uncover and understand the baggage they inherited from their family. Evangelicals have "baggage" from the past as well and an honest look at history is an essential step in correction. In every situation, the people in the portraits that we looked at were raised up by God in a particular historical and cultural moment to bring renewal and revival to the church. Though we face many contemporary challenges, we are reminded through these portraits that the church is God's enterprise. It will always prevail. Finally, our survey of these strategic portraits has broadened our horizon and perspective, reminding us that we are part of a much larger story and family.

---

[1] Francis A. Schaffer, *How Shall We Then Live? The Rise and Decline of Western Thought and Culture,* (Old Tappan, NJ: Fleming H. Revell Company, 1976.

But the hope of this book is that, informed with a greater understanding of our strengths and weaknesses in corporate worship, we may begin to renew and reform our practice in order to fulfill the Kingdom mission that God has given to us in *our* historical moment. It should be evident to all Evangelicals that the Western Church needs to cultivate more rigorous discipleship to meet the challenge of an ever-increasingly hostile and secular culture. Corporate worship, I believe, is the place to start.

We began our historical journey with a broad sweep, surveying people and developments from the New Testament era leading up to the Reformation that influenced the way we worship today. Though the focus of this project is on evangelical Protestant worship, we are, nevertheless, influenced by our ancient forebears probably more than we realize. Christian corporate worship didn't just happen in the last five hundred years. This project would not have been complete without a foundational understanding of our deepest roots.

The debate between Luther and Zwingli was the first singular portrait that we focused on in our consideration of renewing our practice of the Lord's Table. One does not need to embrace a change in substance (transubstantiation or consubstantiation) to understand that Jesus is uniquely present at the Table. Communion is best understood as the Christian Passover where the believer takes part through active remembrance in the fullness of the Christ Event. Such an understanding and regular practice of the Lord's Table provides nourishment, not as salvation, but in spiritual formation as we consider that we have died, risen, and are seated with Christ in the heavenly places (Eph. 2:6).

The picture of German Pietism as shown in the life of August Herman Franke is mostly unknown to American Evangelicals. It is an unfortunate gap in our historical knowledge as Franke embodied most of the values and practices that modern Evangelicals embrace. But Pietism also had a negative outcome, especially when combined with the American culture of individualism. American Pietism has the tendency to become too focused on the individual with the neglect of God's greater mission and work. Individualism has weakened the corporate church and the spiritual formation of the individual believer. Our narcissistic bent is especially expressed in our worship songs that are saturated with personal pronouns. Suggested corrective initiatives begin with cultivating awareness of our self-focused bent and seeking better balance between corporate and individualistic worship song repertoire.

Turning the page in our portrait book, we viewed Revivalism, exemplified in the work of Dwight Moody and Ira Sankey. Moody and Sankey used all means at their disposal to preach the gospel. They leveraged Moody's business sense and Sankey's expressive artistry to draw large crowds for their evangelistic services. Moody and Sankey, of course, weren't the only mass evangelists in evangelical history. Whitefield and Wesley came 150 years before and a whole train of successful American evangelists followed to this day. Mass evangelism, however, was so successful that it influenced the way that Evangelicals conceived, planned, and led their corporate worship. Sunday worship became modeled after evangelistic services with crowd-pleasing music that "prepared the people to hear the Word of God" and a necessary captivating pulpit presence to engage the people in the sermon. Revivialistic worship is an impoverished model that forfeits the strengths of historic Christian worship with the loss of Scripture readings, significant prayer, and the Table. It also distorts the rightful place of music in spiritual formation and creates an unhealthy model of pastoral leadership. Like the issue of individualism, awareness of the shortcomings of revivalistic worship is the place to start. Other corrective suggestions includ reconsidering the role of music, the preacher, and, especially, the structure of the worship service.

When we came to the portrait of the Jesus People Movement, the images splashed with color as many of the leaders still remain alive and active today. The movement of the late 60's through the mid 70's was significant not only in evangelizing a generation of young Americans but in birthing a new kind of church music and perspective on corporate worship. Contemporary praise and worship music, unlike revival gospel songs, sought to engage people directly *with* God rather than simply "prepare hearts to hear the Word." With their simple texts (in comparison with classic hymns) and multiple repetitions, contemporary praise and worship songs have been the target of a good deal of criticism since they were introduced. But the strength of the new genre is in its ability to engage the emotions of the worshipper. Worshippers who will enter into the affect of the song will realize the enrichment the new form has brought to the church. That is not to say, however, that worship leaders should not be cautious in their employment of the new songs. As a popular genre, contemporary praise and worship songs are subject to poorly-conceived theology, romanticism, and to contextual cultural maladies such as narcissism and consumerism. Worship leaders should embrace the new form but proceed with caution and discernment.

The portrait of the Seeker Church Movement represented the apex of revivalism in the local church and the juvenilization of American Christianity. While the motives of the movement were good – namely, going "all in" to evangelize "unchurched Harry and Mary" – the influence that seeker churches had on many other Evangelicals was detrimental. The Seeker Movement, probably more than any other influence, brought consumerism into the church and made it a virtue. The result has been disastrous, cultivating a generation of religious consumers and swapping high production entertainment values for Spirit-empowered worship. Since the turn of the century, the Seeker Movement has been the target of significant evangelical criticism even while megachurches continue to grow. Correctives for a more biblically faithful and spiritually fruitful worship paradigm are to be found in revisiting the biblical nature of the church and its mission.

Components of Renewal

Worship renewal is hard work. There are no "quick fixes." It takes clear vision, hard work, and persistence. Renewalists are, by nature, counter-cultural. They are salmon swimming against the cultural flood. In my own efforts at worship renewal, I've experienced a good deal of frustration along with some growth and progress. Along the way, I've learned a few components that are necessary if worship renewal in a local church is to bear fruit.

As a spiritual endeavor, vital personal and corporate prayer and reflection are essential throughout the effort.

Anyone who has been a leader in the church knows the importance of trust. Trust is the currency with which ministry is done. Establishing trust is where any change in the local church must begin. Worship values and practices are deeply engrained and difficult to shift. The "worship wars" phenomenon of the late twentieth century demonstrated the difficulty of changing worship in an established congregation. Understanding the challenge then, it is vitally important that worship renewalists earn the trust of their people before they begin to make significant changes. If the leader is newly called to a professional position in worship leadership in a church, some changes may be made at the beginning if they were discussed and expected in the interviewing process. But wise leaders will move carefully and make sure ample trust has been built between them and the congregation. As the "currency of ministry," trust is earned in many ways: through time, excellence in job performance, pastoral care, and consistency in Christ-like character. When a leader attempts to change worship paradigms and practices, a large amount of trust is drawn. The wise leader will be sure that there is ample "trust currency" in his account so he won't be "overdrawn."

Once a growing account of trust has been built, the worship renewalist must focus attention on the leadership of the church. This understanding is critical if the people are to follow any path towards renewal. In the center of the leadership core is the senior or lead pastor. A church may have a worship director or pastor on staff, but the reality is that the senior pastor is the primary worship leader of the congregation. They will follow his or her lead, good or bad. I have always found this to be the case in my career as a worship pastor. I could never lead the congregation beyond the understanding and the practice of the senior pastor. It is the reality of leadership dynamics in the local church. The effective worship renewalist will begin efforts in raising awareness and possibilities through interaction with the senior pastor. Inviting the pastor to a worship conference is a great way to begin the conversation. Reading books together on worship renewal would also be an effective way to move forward. In my efforts in worship renewal, I have tried to bring about change without first getting the senior pastor on board. I've worked with worship teams, choir, study groups, and even the staff. But the results were always less than what I had hoped for if I did not recruit the senior pastor's support first. You cannot lead beyond his or her influence. In fact, it would be far more effective if the senior pastor would lead the way in changing the worship paradigms and practice with the renewalist serving as consultant and support.

Depending on the governance dynamics of the church (staff or board-led), the senior pastor and worship renewalist can begin to influence the primary leaders of the church. Book discussion groups and retreats are effective ways to begin to build awareness of the need for renewal and possible steps forward. It is important, however, to realize that not all church leaders are eager to grow and learn. In that case, it may require patience until a leadership core that is more willing to learn is in place. That may happen through the typical cycles of board transition or the pastor and renewalist may invest personal time to encourage those who resist change. This is a difficult challenge, but enlisting lay leadership in the worship renewal process is essential if it is to succeed. It may even be necessary to propose higher standards for church leadership through by-law changes. I believe every church leader should be eager to grow and learn if the congregation is to be vital. Renewalists need a core of life-long learners in the congregation that will understand and support their efforts.

Throughout my ministry career, I have been a solo-planner of corporate worship. I've gathered the essential elements from participants, such as sermon titles and texts as well as any other things beyond my personal direction. I have then added the worship elements for which I was responsible and crafted the service into a flowing conversation. Such an approach is marvelously efficient. Since crafting a worship service is an art, solo-planning also tends to result in a more cohesive order and experience.

But while solo-planning is efficient, it also restricts the creativity of the worship service to the imagination of one person. Moreover, if the worship planner is trying to initiate change, he or she will be on their own. No one else will share the vision or the rationale for renewal initiatives. Unfortunately, I have found that some of the changes that I have effectively brought to churches did not last beyond my tenure. There is a better, though more challenging way. In their helpful and practical book, *Designing Worship Together,* Norma deWaal Malyeft and Howard Vanderwell suggest utilizing a worship planning team made up of the preaching pastor, the chief musician, and a diversity of invested lay people.[2] The strength of the team-planning model is the combined diverse imagination of the members. The challenges are many: finding time to meet, securing the time commitment from each member, and "getting on the same page." Malyeft and Vanderwell suggest meeting monthly rather than weekly. Perhaps most helpful of all, they suggest including an educational component to the monthly planning meeting to form the group's biblical, theological, and cultural imagination. Such a model could be very effective in bringing about incremental worship renewal to the congregation over time.

Finally, it is very important to prepare and educate the congregation as changes to their worship practice are initiated. It is my experience that most people in every church want to be led. They will respond to good leadership that respects and loves them. Out of respect and love, then, effective worship renwalists will affirm the heritage and values of their congregation while providing vision and rationale for changes that are being implemented. Failure to affirm and explain will inevitably lead to reaction and rejection of the leader's efforts. For example, if a new practice of the Lord's Table is being implemented, clear biblical teaching must be provided to the people as to why the changes are being made and the spiritual benefits that will result. If the style of worship music is being changed or expanded, a compelling biblical and cultural justification should be provided. Patience, love, and respect from leadership to the people are essential if worship renewal is to take root and bear fruit.

---

[2] Norma deWaal Malyft and Howard Vanderwell, *Designing Worship Together: Models and Strategies for Worship Planning,* (Herndon, VA: The Alban Institute, 2005).

Streams of Worship Renewal

There is no doubt that worship renewal is a growing trend among today's Evangelicals. What the Praise and Worship Movement brought in awareness, thirty years of change and reflection have planted seeds for more spiritually transformative worship paradigms. Even my own denominational Baptist tribe is considering how we should now worship, given the challenges of a weakened American Church in the Twenty-First Century.[3] Such a trend among Baptists is remarkable because we have tended to shun church traditions and rely on our own contemporary interpretations of Scripture and the Faith. Late author and founding editor of the Religion Department of *Publishers Weekly*, Phyllis Tickle, posited that there would be a great reimagining of churches at this point in history. We are at the 500th Anniversary of the Protestant Reformation. In her words, now is the time for a "rummage sale" of old paradigms and a re-emergence of an effective church for a new day.[4] Perhaps. The "Emerging Church Movement" that began in the early years of the new century that challenged the status quo in most evangelical churches represents another impulse of worship renewal. Remarkably, many emerging churches embraced ancient worship practices of the early Church Fathers.[5] And while the emerging church impulse has waned, the lasting impact of the questions that the movement asked remains. As we near the third decade of the new century, the reality of growing ethnic diversity especially within American urban contexts presents the exciting opportunity and growing field of multi-cultural worship within our local churches.[6]

---

[3] Rodney Wallace Kennedy and Dereck C. Hatch, eds., *Gathering Together: Baptists at Work in Worship,* (Eugene, OR: Pickwick Publications, 2013).

[4] Phyllis Tickle, *The Great Emergence: How Christianity is Changing and Why,* (Grand Rapids: Baker Books, 2008, 2012).

[5] Dan Kimball, *Emerging Worship: Creating Worship Gatherings for New Generations,* (El Cajon, CA: emergentYS Books, 2004).

[6] Sandra Maria Van Opstal, *The Next Worship: Glorifying God in a Diverse World,* (Downers Grove: Intervarsity Press Books, 2016).

Before he died in 2007, worship renewalist Robert E. Webber was a champion of Millennials. He promoted the thought of Neil Howe and William Strauss who suggested that, like their grandparents, the Builders (WWII Generation), Millennials would play a very positive and courageous role in cultural transformation.[7] Webber also noticed the dissatisfaction of Millennials towards their Boomer parents' consumer values and held out hope for a new generation that would embrace ancient worship practices with contemporary cultural relevance.[8] For good or for ill, Millennials are the emerging leaders who will bear the burden of shepherding the church into the future. Like Webber, I choose to be optimistic about what they will bring.

During the last forty years, there is probably no one who has been more influential in American worship renewal than Robert Webber. He was born into a fundamentalist missionary's home and graduated from Bob Jones University. He earned graduate degrees from Anglican, Presbyterian, and Lutheran schools. He would eventually land at Wheaton College where he was a beloved and provocative professor of theology for over thirty years. His interests eventually led him to a passionate study and appreciation of the early church. His study and reflection led him to embrace a more historic practice of worship, chronicled in his book, *Evangelicals on the Canterbury Trail.*[9] But Webber's interests extended far beyond denominationalism to a life-calling of worship renewal within the broader evangelical church. Webber was an extremely prolific author, writing over forty books, developing a worship curriculum, editing an eight-volume reference set, and writing countless articles and media material on worship. He was instrumental in bringing together hundreds of evangelical theologians and leaders to issue *The Chicago Call* in

---

[7] Neil Howe and William Strauss, *Millennials Rising: The Next Generation,* (New York: Vintage Books, 2000) and *The Fourth Turning* (New York: Broadway Books, 1997).

[8] Robert E. Webber, *The Younger Evangelicals: Facing the Challenges of the New World,* (Grand Rapids: Baker Books, 2000).

[9] Robert E. Webber, *Evangelicals on the Canterbury Trail: Why Evangelicals Are Attracted to the Liturgical Church* (Waco, TX: Word Books, 1985).

1977 and *The Call to an Ancient-Evangelical Future* in 2006.[10] Both documents urge renewal in the contemporary church from early church perspective and praxis.

But perhaps Webber's most lasting legacy will be the school that bears his name and carries his vision: The Robert E. Webber Institute for Worship Studies in Jacksonville, Florida.[11] I began attending the school in January, 2001. I felt like it was designed just for me. I had a good biblical foundation, a graduate degree in music, and had been passionately engaged in worship ministry for over twenty years. IWS offered the only doctoral degree program that fit my profile. And it fit me "to a tee." As I have explained along the way, I learned and grew a lot through my time at the Institute. It changed me. Graduates are fond of saying "it ruined me." The school broke many of my presuppositions and reformed my perspective. Though the cost was far less than most graduate theological schools (I completed the program with no debt while also paying for my son's undergraduate degree), I was deeply enriched. For those who feel called to worship renewal, I can recommend no other better pathway than The Robert E. Webber Institute for Worship Studies.

An anonymous author has written, "The past leads us to the present and the present leads to the future, therefore, it is impossible to build the future without knowing the past." This book has been my humble contribution towards that task. We live in challenging times. We cannot tell what kind of portrait we are making of ourselves. That is for later generations to discern. But from what we have seen in our historical journey, we must follow in the train of our predecessors with the same focus and perseverance for the Kingdom. God will revive and nurture his church. Still, we are called to be stewards of the time that has been given to us. May God grant us the wisdom and courage to follow our Lord Jesus Christ into the future. The renewal of corporate worship, I believe, is the place we must begin.

---

[10] *The Call to an Ancient-Evangelical Future* is included in this book as Appendix B. You can also find more information here: https://www.ancientfuturefaithnetwork.org/the-call/

[11] www.iws.edu

APPENDIX A
CREATING FLOW IN A WORSHIP SET

Corporate worship is relational. It is like a conversation. It must go somewhere. It begins with God's initiation and continues through cycles of his revelation and our response. Those who design services must understand the relational and conversational dynamics of worship. This short piece addresses worship flow through song sets, but the same principles apply to the design of the entire worship service including prayers, sermon, and sacraments.

Theological Thread

There must be a theological thread of thought that is connected throughout the worship set. It may be of a singular theme or it may be a series of interconnected theological thoughts that segue from one to the next.

Many worship planners insist that the set be planned around one singular theme. That idea is fine for some situations, but it is not a scriptural injunction. It is also limiting. Think of a typical conversation. The subject matter may be on one issue, but frequently it is one big idea with several interrelated tangents. One idea bounces off the previous idea. Look at Jesus' discussion with the woman at the well in John 4. He asks her for a drink. She responds in surprise to His initiation. He tells her of living water, but then completely changes the subject to her personal life – her "love life." She changes the subject again to worship. Jesus turns the conversation back to his identity as the Messiah. One idea springs from the previous, but Jesus masterfully keeps the conversation on point without being superficial.

Our worship planning should deal with theological issues in the same way. With theologically informed and creative thinking, a good worship leader sees the interlinking threads and guides the people in the "worship conversation." Most importantly, a worship planner and leader understands the progression of worship.

One model of worship progression is found in Isaiah 6:1-8, where the prophet has an encounter with the Holy God. God initiates the vision with a revelation of His holiness. The prophet responds in confession of his unworthiness. God provides cleansing and forgiveness and then issues a call. The prophet, having seen the Holy God and having his sins purged, responds to God's invitation. Throughout the encounter, there is a natural progression of activity. A skilled worship planner will look for and facilitate this natural progression of revelation and response.

Another model of worship progression can be found in Psalm 95:1-8. The psalmist offers an invitation to exuberant worship in verses one and two. Verses three through five reveal (or remind) the worshippers of God's mighty acts in and over the Cosmos. Having come joyfully into God's presence and being reminded of His mighty acts, the worshipper is then invited to worship humbly and bow down before the Lord. The nurturing relationship between God and His people is reinforced through the metaphor of Shepherd and sheep. The psalm closes with a solemn warning to hear and heed God's voice.

Both Isaiah 6 and Psalm 95 are scriptural models of the worship relational dynamic. They are not necessarily a formula to reproduce, although they do illustrate natural flow in the revelation/response conversation. Charismatic worship leaders have captured the idea of progression in worship with different phases drawn from Psalm 95:

> *Invitation:* "Let us sing for joy ... shout aloud."
> *Engagement:* "Let us come before him with thanksgiving."
> *Exaltation:* "For the Lord is the great God ... the mountain peaks belong to him."
> *Adoration:* "Come, let us bow down ... let us kneel."

Intimacy: "For we are the people of his pasture, the flock under his care."[1]

Theological thread, then, is the linking of conversational thought within a worship experience. Transitions are essential. Sometimes one song will lead naturally into the next. The subject of the earlier lyric suggests (or demands) the response of the lyric that follows. Often, one song can flow into the next without any comment. Occasionally, a few words or a prayer will help to connect the ideas. Some skilled worship leaders are able to make those comments or prayers through improvised melodies and lyrics.

As the five phases above suggest, be sure that your worship song set goes somewhere in its theological thought. It must have a sense of journey and home.

Where do the ideas come from with which to build a worship set? Typically, the central idea comes from the sermon topic. But worship leaders do not need to say the same thing that the preacher is saying. It may be even more effective to address a complementary theological issue to set up the sermon. For example, if the preacher is addressing sin, the worship leader may plan the set around the holiness of God to give a contrast and context for the issue. Sometimes, preachers can be very difficult and preach about bioethics or nuclear proliferation. The worship leader must then explore theological topics that address the deeper issues of the sermon topic. Of course, the preacher may be helpful here.

Other settings do not call for a sermon, such as prayer services, devotionals, solemn assemblies, etc... In those settings, it is best to explore with the leaders of the event what might be the most critical spiritual issues of the gathered people. Pastoral insight is very helpful in these settings.

Song sets don't have to be all on one theme. But they should have some central organizing idea around which all other thoughts are connected.

---

[1] Barry Liesch, "A Structure Runs Through It,"
<http://www.christianitytoday.com/bcl/areas/worship/articles/100405.html>

Affective Development

The emotions of worship ebb and flow. Without being manipulative (forcing emotional response from people), the worship leader should be aware of the potential emotional impact of each song in the set. The worship "journey" or conversation should be planned with these "hills and valleys" in mind. Music that tends to reinforce a high level of enthusiasm or periods of contemplation generally should not be sustained over long periods of time. Exceptions to this concept are worship experiences specifically designed as celebrations or solemn assemblies. When the musical affect remains the same, two negative results occur. First, the people will become emotionally exhausted. Second, the affect is devalued because there is no contrasting emotion. Life consists of ups and downs. Our worship experience should as well. Psalm 95 is an excellent model of celebration and contemplation.

The five phases of worship also illustrate affective development. Invitation through exaltation demonstrates a rising celebrative engagement. Adoration and intimacy are more reflective. Each phase of worship is not necessarily equal in time (or number of songs) with the others. But the journey through each represents a logical theological flow as well as emotional progression. The responsible worship leader does not force the people to respond in a particular way. Rather, the set is planned to facilitate the free flow the Holy Spirit through a path that is modeled in Scripture and makes relational/conversational sense.

Musical Mechanics

Music is the "track" that theological thought and emotion runs on in the worship set. Tempo, groove, and key relate to affective development. A good tune and rhythmic groove will effectively carry the theological thought of the lyric. The musical challenge for the worship leader is to facilitate transitions that will create effective segues from one theological thought to the next between songs. Affective transitions must also be facilitated in the same way. The worship conversation should flow and continue without distraction.

There are several musical devices that can help facilitate the journey:

Spontaneous congregational applause. This is not a musical device at all. But it can be an effective bridge from one song to the next. The applause distracts from the musical key and groove associations from one song to the next. Just go right into the following song.

No transition. Sometimes two songs are in the same key and same grove. Just move on to the next song.

Related key relationships. You can go from one song to the next if the second key is a fourth higher than the previous key (provided that the first song is in a major key – otherwise make the last chord major). This is a dominant-tonic or V-I relationship. (For example, from D to G.) Sometimes, you can also effectively go up a half-step or whole step without modulating chords. Going from major to relative or parallel minor (C to Am or C to Cm) can also be effective without transition chords. Nuance, however, is essential. Sometimes you will need to be subtle, winding down the musical momentum before shifting, or it can be dramatic and sudden.

Modulation. If you are going from one key that is distant from the previous key, you may need to find a modulation formula. That formula will almost always end with the last chord being the V of the new key. Look for common tones between chords. Keyboards are usually the most effective in doing these kinds of modulations.

Rhythmic groove change. You will need to think this through. Some songs are in the same groove as the previous – go right into it. Other's demand a dramatic break. A drummer's "click" on the sticks can be effective, especially in up-tempo songs. Sometimes, you will need to let the rhythmic groove wind down: vamp on the closing chord progression while bringing down instrumentation, energy, and eventually tempo. Establishing a new groove by playing through the first verse or chorus without vocals can be effective in establishing not only a new musical feel, but also preparing the people for a new theological thread.

Evaluative Questions

1. What is the central theological idea to the set?

2. Do the ideas flow from one to the next? Do they flow naturally, or do they need short transitional statements or prayers to keep the people focused together on the thought? If the spoken word is used, will there be musical accompaniment underlying the words?

3. Is there real theological progression that reflects the idea of revelation/response?

4. Is there sense of emotional journey? Not just up and down, but destination and arrival?

5. Does the music carry the theological ideas well?

6. Are the musical transitions effective in moving the thought and affect forward without distraction?

APPENDIX B
THE CALL TO AN ANCIENT EVANGLICAL FUTURE

I have included this document as an appendix to the book because it suggests "tracks to run on" for renewal in the Twenty-First Century Evangelical Church. While only point four specifically mentions corporate worship, all six themes do have direct correlation to worship renewal. Robert E. Webber spearheaded the initiative in 2006 with the collaboration of over 300 theologians, pastors, and other church leaders. The Ancient Future Faith Network (linked at the end of the document) exists to further the intention of the AEF Call.

PROLOGUE

In every age the Holy Spirit calls the Church to examine its faithfulness to God's revelation in Jesus Christ, authoritatively recorded in Scripture and handed down through the Church. Thus, while we affirm the global strength and vitality of worldwide Evangelicalism in our day, we believe the North American expression of Evangelicalism needs to be especially sensitive to the new external and internal challenges facing God's people.

These external challenges include the current cultural milieu and the resurgence of religious and political ideologies. The internal challenges include Evangelical accommodation to civil religion, rationalism, privatism and pragmatism. In light of these challenges, we call Evangelicals to strengthen their witness through a recovery of the faith articulated by the consensus of the ancient Church and its guardians in the traditions of Eastern Orthodoxy, Roman Catholicism, the Protestant Reformation and the Evangelical awakenings. Ancient Christians faced a world of paganism, Gnosticism and political domination. In the face of heresy and persecution, they understood history through Israel's story, culminating in the death and resurrection of Jesus and the coming of God's Kingdom.

Today, as in the ancient era, the Church is confronted by a host of master narratives that contradict and compete with the gospel. The pressing question is: who gets to narrate the world? The Call to an Ancient Evangelical Future challenges Evangelical Christians to restore the priority of the divinely inspired biblical story of God's acts in history. The narrative of God's Kingdom holds eternal implications for the mission of the Church, its theological reflection, its public ministries of worship and spirituality and its life in the world. By engaging these themes, we believe the Church will be strengthened to address the issues of our day.

1. ON THE PRIMACY OF THE BIBLICAL NARRATIVE

We call for a return to the priority of the divinely authorized canonical story of the Triune God. This story-Creation, Incarnation, and Re-creation-was effected by Christ's recapitulation of human history and summarized by the early Church in its Rules of Faith. The gospel-formed content of these Rules served as the key to the interpretation of Scripture and its critique of contemporary culture, and thus shaped the church's pastoral ministry. Today, we call Evangelicals to turn away from modern theological methods that reduce the gospel to mere propositions, and from contemporary pastoral ministries so compatible with culture that they camouflage God's story or empty it of its cosmic and redemptive meaning. In a world of competing stories, we call Evangelicals to recover the truth of God's word as the story of the world, and to make it the centerpiece of Evangelical life.

2. ON THE CHURCH, THE CONTINUATION OF GOD'S NARRATIVE

We call Evangelicals to take seriously the visible character of the Church. We call for a commitment to its mission in the world in fidelity to God's mission (*Missio Dei*), and for an exploration of the ecumenical implications this has for the unity, holiness, catholicity, and apostolicity of the Church. Thus, we call Evangelicals to turn away from an individualism that makes the Church a mere addendum to God's redemptive plan. Individualistic Evangelicalism has contributed to the current problems of churchless Christianity, redefinitions of the Church according to business models, separatist ecclesiologies and judgmental attitudes toward the Church. Therefore, we call Evangelicals to recover their place in the community of the Church catholic.

3. ON THE CHURCH'S THEOLOGICAL REFLECTION ON GOD'S NARRATIVE

We call for the Church's reflection to remain anchored in the Scriptures in continuity with the theological interpretation learned from the early Fathers. Thus, we call Evangelicals to turn away from methods that separate theological reflection from the common traditions of the Church. These modern methods compartmentalize God's story by analyzing its separate parts, while ignoring God's entire redemptive work as recapitulated in Christ. Anti-historical attitudes also disregard the common biblical and theological legacy of the ancient Church. Such disregard ignores the hermeneutical value of the Church's ecumenical creeds. This reduces God's story of the world to one of many competing theologies and impairs the unified witness of the Church to God's plan for the history of the world. Therefore, we call Evangelicals to unity in "the tradition that has been believed everywhere, always and by all," as well as to humility and charity in their various Protestant traditions.

4. ON THE CHURCH'S WORSHIP AS TELLING AND ENACTING GOD'S NARRATIVE

We call for public worship that sings, preaches and enacts God's story. We call for a renewed consideration of how God ministers to us in baptism, Eucharist, confession, the laying on of hands, marriage, healing and through the charisms of the Spirit, for these actions shape our lives and signify the meaning of the world. Thus, we call Evangelicals to turn away from forms of worship that focus on God as a mere object of the intellect or that assert the self as the source of worship. Such worship has resulted in lecture-oriented, music-driven, performance-centered and program-controlled models that do not adequately proclaim God's cosmic redemption. Therefore, we call Evangelicals to recover the historic substance of worship of Word and Table and to attend to the Christian year, which marks time according to God's saving acts.

5. ON SPIRITUAL FORMATION IN THE CHURCH AS EMBODIMENT OF GOD'S NARRATIVE

We call for a catechetical spiritual formation of the people of God that is based firmly on a Trinitarian biblical narrative. We are concerned when spirituality is separated from the story of God and baptism into the life of Christ and his Body. Spirituality, made independent from God's story, is often characterized by legalism, mere intellectual knowledge, an overly therapeutic culture, New Age Gnosticism, a dualistic rejection of this world and a narcissistic preoccupation with one's own experience. These false spiritualities are inadequate for the challenges we face in today's world. Therefore, we call Evangelicals to return to a historic spirituality like that taught and practiced in the ancient catechumenate.

6. ON THE CHURCH'S EMBODIED LIFE IN THE WORLD

We call for a cruciform holiness and commitment to God's mission in the world. This embodied holiness affirms life, biblical morality and appropriate self-denial. It calls us to be faithful stewards of the created order and bold prophets to our contemporary culture. Thus, we call Evangelicals to intensify their prophetic voice against forms of indifference to God's gift of life, economic and political injustice, ecological insensitivity and the failure to champion the poor and marginalized. Too often we have failed to stand prophetically against the culture's captivity to racism, consumerism, political correctness, civil religion, sexism, ethical relativism, violence and the culture of death. These failures have muted the voice of Christ to the world through his Church and detract from God's story of the world, which the Church is collectively to embody. Therefore, we call the Church to recover its counter-cultural mission to the world.

EPILOGUE

In sum, we call Evangelicals to recover the conviction that God's story shapes the mission of the Church to bear witness to God's Kingdom and to inform the spiritual foundations of civilization. We set forth this Call as an ongoing, open-ended conversation. We are aware that we have our blind spots and weaknesses. Therefore, we encourage Evangelicals to engage this Call within educational centers, denominations and local churches through publications and conferences.

We pray that we can move with intention to proclaim a loving, transcendent, triune God who has become involved in our history. In line with Scripture, creed and tradition, it is our deepest desire to embody God's purposes in the mission of the Church through our theological reflection, our worship, our spirituality and our life in the world, all the while proclaiming that Jesus is Lord over all creation.

This Call is issued in the spirit of *sic et non*; therefore those who affix their names to this Call need not agree with all its content. Rather, its consensus is that these are issues to be discussed in the tradition of *semper reformanda* as the church faces the new challenges of our time. Over a period of seven months, more than 300 persons have participated via e-mail to write The Call. These men and women represent a broad diversity of ethnicity and denominational affiliation. The four theologians who most consistently interacted with the development of The Call have been named as Theological Editors. The Board of Reference was given the special assignment of overall approval.

https://www.ancientfuturefaithnetwork.org/the-call/
02.21.2017

Made in the USA
Coppell, TX
30 March 2021

52677246R00125